David Beckham

Other books in the People in the News series:

people in the NEWS

David Beckham

by Michael V. Uschan

LUCENT BOOKS
A part of Gale, Cengage Learning

GALE
CENGAGE Learning

Detroit • New York • San Francisco • New Haven, Conn • Waterville, Maine • London

GALE
CENGAGE Learning

LIBRARY OF CONGRESS CATALOGING-IN-PUBLICATION DATA

Uschan, Michael V., 1948-
  David Beckham / by Michael V. Uschan.
    p. cm. — (People in the news)
  Includes bibliographical references and index.
  ISBN 978-1-4205-0054-7 (hardcover)
1. Beckham, David, 1975—Juvenile literature. 2. Soccer players—England—
Biography—Juvenile literature. 3. Celebrities—England—Biography—Juvenile literature.
I. Title.
  GV942.7.B432U83 2008
   796.334092—dc22
   [B]
                                                      2008002561

Lucent Books
27500 Drake Rd
Farmington Hills MI 48331

ISBN-13: 978-1-4205-0054-7
ISBN-10: 1-4205-0054-6

Printed in the United States of America
1 2 3 4 5 6 7 12 11 10 09 08

Contents

ame and celebrity are alluring. People are drawn to those who walk in fame's spotlight, whether they are known for great accomplishments or for notorious deeds. The lives of the famous pique public interest and attract attention, perhaps because their experiences seem in some ways so different from, yet in other ways so similar to, our own.

Newspapers, magazines, and television regularly capitalize on this fascination with celebrity by running profiles of famous people. For example, television programs such as *Entertainment Tonight* devote all their programming to stories about entertainment and entertainers. Magazines such as *People* fill their pages with stories of the private lives of famous people. Even newspapers, newsmagazines, and television news frequently delve into the lives of well-known personalities. Despite the number of articles and programs, few provide more than a superficial glimpse at their subjects.

Lucent's People in the News series offers young readers a deeper look into the lives of today's newsmakers, the influences that have shaped them, and the impact they have had in their fields of endeavor and on other people's lives. The subjects of the series hail from many disciplines and walks of life. They include authors, musicians, athletes, political leaders, entertainers, entrepreneurs, and others who have made a mark on modern life and who, in many cases, will continue to do so for years to come.

These biographies are more than factual chronicles. Each book emphasizes the contributions, accomplishments, or deeds that have brought fame or notoriety to the individual and shows how that person has influenced modern life. Authors portray their subjects in a realistic, unsentimental light. For example, Bill Gates —the cofounder and chief executive officer of the software giant Microsoft—has been instrumental in making personal computers the most vital tool of the modern age. Few dispute his business savvy, his perseverance, or his technical expertise, yet critics say he is ruthless in his dealings with competitors and driven more by his desire to maintain Microsoft's dominance in the computer industry than by an interest in furthering technology.

In these books, young readers will encounter inspiring stories about real people who achieved success despite enormous obstacles. Oprah Winfrey—the most powerful, most watched, and wealthiest woman on television today—spent the first six years of her life in the care of her grandparents while her unwed mother sought work and a better life elsewhere. Her adolescence was colored by promiscuity, pregnancy at age fourteen, rape, and sexual abuse.

Each author documents and supports his or her work with an array of primary and secondary source quotations taken from diaries, letters, speeches, and interviews. All quotes are footnoted to show readers exactly how and where biographers derive their information and provide guidance for further research. The quotations enliven the text by giving readers eyewitness views of the life and accomplishments of each person covered in the People in the News series.

In addition, each book in the series includes photographs, annotated bibliographies, timelines, and comprehensive indexes. For both the casual reader and the student researcher, the People in the News series offers insight into the lives of today's newsmakers—people who shape the way we live, work, and play in the modern age.

David Beckham: A Soccer Star and World Celebrity

John Carlin went to Africa in June 2003 to research facts for an article on the AIDS epidemic there. Much to his amazement, almost everyone the English freelance writer met in Kenya was more interested in talking about soccer star David Beckham than the dreaded disease he had come to investigate. Manchester United, a professional English team, had recently sold Beckham to Spain's Real Madrid for $50 million. The intensity of the interest that Kenyans displayed about Beckham convinced Carlin, who had worked extensively as a sportswriter covering soccer, that he should write a book about the soccer star. In the introduction to *White Angels: Beckham, Real Madrid and the New Football*, Carlin writes that "I shouldn't have been surprised" that Beckham's departure from the famed English team created so much excitement:

> Barely a week had passed since what would turn out to be—with the arguable exception of the outbreak of war in Iraq—the news story with the greatest global impact of 2003: the transfer of the world's most glamorous footballer [soccer player] to the world's most glamorous club.[1]

Beckham's move to Spain was an important global news item because Beckham was the most famous player in the world's most popular sport, one that is known in most of the world as football

David Beckham is considered to be one of the most famous sports figures in the world.

or association football, the latter being its formal name. In the United States and Canada, however, it is called soccer, a slang term derived from "assoc.," the abbreviation of *association*. The story of Beckham's sale to Real Madrid was given little news media coverage in the United States because soccer is not a major sport in that country. But in June 2007 when Beckham left Real Madrid to play for yet another team, U.S. television stations and newspapers devoted extensive coverage to the story. The reason was that Beckham's new team was the Los Angeles Galaxy.

Not Famous in the United States

USA Today reporter Ellen Hale once wrote a newspaper story about Beckham in which she claims, "He's the most famous man Americans don't know." Even though Beckham had been one of the world's most famous athletes for more than a decade, he was never a major sports figure in the United States until he started playing for Galaxy. He was so famous that Ellis Cashmore, a professor of culture, media, and sports at Staffordshire University in England, wrote a sociological study about how Beckham became a global cultural icon. Cashmore claims that Beckham is one of the most significant athletes to ever play any sport:

> He is the purest sports celebrity in the history of the world. Tiger Woods? Michael Jordan? They redefined their sport, and they are respected. But Beckham has transcended that. He is worshipped. His fan base goes far beyond sports; many of them don't even care about football.[2]

Jordan in basketball and Woods in golf are famous around the world because they are considered to be the greatest athletes to ever play their respective sports. Although soccer historians do not claim Beckham is the finest player his sport has produced, he is more well-known worldwide than either Jordan or Woods. That is because soccer is far more popular in most countries than basketball or golf and because Beckham's fans are not restricted to people who like sports. His appeal to men and women around the globe extends beyond his being an athlete and ranges from his good looks to his wife Victoria, who is famous herself as Posh Spice of the musical group Spice Girls.

Brand Beckham

Beckham is one of the world's highest-paid athletes and in 2006 he earned $33 million. Much of that income came from money he was paid to endorse products like Adidas shoes and sportswear, Pepsi soda, and Gillette razor blades. Matt Haig, an English financial writer, claims that Beckham's global fame makes him such a powerful figure in product endoresments that he has himself become a brand name, one that can automatically help companies increase their sales when it is attached to their products. Haig claims Beckham has this ability because he appeals to so many different types of people. Haig writes:

> Beckham is a brand that speaks to many people. He is a footballer, a fashion icon, a sex symbol, half of a celebrity power

The worldwide fame of David Beckham has provided him with numerous endorsement opportunities, including Adidas shoes.

couple. [He] appeals to a broad section of society and like the most successful brands he is able to cross gender and class lines with apparent ease.[3]

Beckham has millions of fans who have no interest in soccer. Many women like him because he is handsome. When Beckham was introduced to 5,000 Galaxy fans in Carson, California, on

July 13, 2007, fifteen-year-old Alyssa Bricker said she liked him because he was good-looking. "Oh, yeah. He's hot,"[4] she told a newspaper reporter. Gay people admire Beckham because he is one of the few professional athletes who openly accept them; he has even appeared on the cover of *Attitude*, an English gay magazine. Beckham also attracts people interested in fashion even though his tastes can be bizarre—he has admitted that he sometimes wears a sarong. Beckham, however, generally dresses very fashionably. *Vanity Fair* in 2006 named him to a list of the world's best-dressed men that included actor George Clooney and Prince William of England.

People who are entranced by celebrities enjoy reading about Beckham's dramatic lifestyle. That ranges from his latest hairstyle—he has had a Mohawk, cornrows, and a shaved head—to his tattoos, which include the names of his sons Brooklyn, Romeo, and Cruz. Many people are also intrigued that this sports superstar is married to an entertainer who is also famous. The news media have nicknamed the couple "Posh and Becks" and newspapers, magazines, and television shows regularly run stories and pictures about them. There are also many Internet sites devoted to both members of one of the world's most famous couples.

Beckham's "Universal Appeal"

The fact that so many different kinds of people feel a connection to Beckham is a major reason why he is so well-known and popular throughout the world. Mark Lawrenson, a sports commentator for the British Broadcasting Corporation (BBC), believes that nearly everyone can find something to like about Beckham: "He's just got this amazing universal appeal. The men all want to be him, and the women all want to either [date] him or be his mum-in-law."[5]

Chapter 1

A Young Boy Dreams of Soccer Stardom

Eleven-year-old David Beckham had just finished playing soccer for the Ridgeway Rovers, a recreational team that held games every Sunday near his home in Chingford, England. As always, Beckham had been the best player on either team competing, one who was able to run faster and kick the ball straighter and farther than anyone else. But after the game while his mother, Sandra, was talking to him, tears began running down the blond boy's face. Beckham explained years later that they were tears of joy because his mother had just given him some wonderful news: "My mum came up and said, 'It's good that you've played well today, because Manchester United were watching you, and they want you to come down and have a trial.' I just stood there and cried."[6]

Manchester United is one of the world's most famous sports franchises and has an estimated 50 million fans spread around the globe. It was Beckham's favorite team, and he had dreamed of playing professional soccer for Manchester United for as long as he could remember. The early interest the club showed in the young boy's soccer prowess would eventually lead him to become the richest and most famous player soccer has ever had.

Growing Up a Footballer

David Robert Joseph Beckham was born on May 2, 1975, in Leytonstone, a working-class suburb in the northeastern part of London, England. His parents were David Edward Alan "Ted" Beckham, an appliance repairman, and Sandra Georgina West, a hairdresser, and he has two sisters—Lynne and Joanne. Soon after David was born, his family moved to Chingford, another section of London's east end. It was there that David first begin playing the sport that would make him world famous.

In the United States, many small children start throwing around baseballs and footballs before they can even walk. Since soccer is the most popular sport in England, it was natural that David would grow up learning to play that game. Ted Beckham began

David Beckham grew up loving Manchester United. His family would travel a long distance to watch Manchester when he was a child.

teaching David to play soccer not long after his son began walking. "I used to throw a rolled-up sock at him so he could practice kicking," Beckham said.[7] The proud father still has a video of David doing that when he was just three years old. Naturally, the toddler was wearing a tiny replica of the uniform of Manchester United, the family's favorite team.

David came to love Manchester United because his parents did. The whole family would travel to Manchester to watch games even though it was 200 miles (322km) north of London. Because Manchester competed against teams based in and near London, it was not always easy for the young boy to root for Manchester, whose nickname was the Red Devils. As an adult, Beckham once explained how his friends and classmates at school often harassed him because of his allegiance to the northern team:

> I've always been a Man United fan and I always will be. I got [ridiculed] horrendously at school, especially when Arsenal or Tottenham [two other top professional teams] beat us, which at the time was quite a bit. Mind you there was a more memorable time when we beat Arsenal 6–2 so that went down well. I made sure I wore my United shirt to school that day.[8]

The youngster, however, was not content with being just a fan. Someone asked David, when he was still very young, what he wanted to be when he grew up. He immediately responded "A famous footballer [soccer player]."[9] His father did all he could to help his son accomplish that lofty goal.

Like Father, Like Son

When David was only four years old, his father began taking him to Chase Lane Park nearly every day to practice soccer. Ted Beckham did not have his son kick the ball around aimlessly or play pretend games in which David would always win. Instead, he helped David perfect basic soccer techniques such as stopping the ball, controlling it carefully as he ran with it down the field, and kicking it into the goal to score a point.

David's father, Ted Beckham, helped him perfect his soccer skills at a young age.

The endless drills were similar to those the elder Beckham had learned as a youngster while nurturing the same dream his son now had of becoming a professional player. Although Ted Beckham had been a promising young player and even had a tryout with a professional team, he had never been good enough to play professionally. He had to quit school when he was fifteen years old to work as a hotel waiter in order to support himself, but he continued playing recreational soccer. When David was born, he decided to help his son become a great player, something his own father had not been able to do for him. "He was working,

A Father Trains His Son

Ted Beckham explains how he taught his son basic soccer skills and pushed him hard to become a good player. Beckham writes:

> I watch David playing now and see things we did over the park together in the early days, and it gives me such a big thrill. You've got to have the right materials to work with, and I certainly did when I was coaching David. When he was a boy it was just football, football, football. And when you get a response from somebody, you work harder with them. That's what I did with David. He didn't take a lot of working with because he was a good little kid. We were more than father and son, we were best mates. On a Sunday, after young David had played football, he'd have a bath and dinner, then we'd settle down to watch football on TV. Midweek, he would rush home from school, do his homework and then say, "Dad, let's watch football." We'd sit and watch videos together and analyze games.

Ted Beckham, "Becks the Unseen Pictures: I'm So Proud of My David," *Daily Mirror* (London), September 19, 2005, p. 2.

money was tight and he would watch me play sometimes, but that was it,"[10] Ted Beckham has said of his own father.

Ted, however, was never too busy to help David learn the game they both loved. As an adult, Beckham remembers how serious his father was in the way in which he taught him soccer:

Practice, practice, practice. You could always find him and me over at the park kicking a ball at each other. I just wanted to shoot at him and score, but he worked on all aspects of my game, especially ball control and passing using my weaker left foot.[11]

Ted Beckham is not the first father to try and help his son realize the dream of sports glory that had eluded him. And like the father of another world famous athlete—Earl Woods, who helped Tiger Woods become the greatest golfer in that sport's history—he was demanding and could often be harsh in his desire to see his son excel. "I was pretty hard on David in many ways," Ted Beckham has said. "There were lots of times when I made him cry, but it's all come out good. That was part of learning."[12] Even though some practice sessions were tough on the young boy, Beckham is grateful for what his father did for him: "I suppose you could say he was pushing me along. You'd also have to say, though, that it was all I wanted to do and I was lucky Dad was so willing to do it with me."[13] The father-and-son practice sessions helped David perfect basic soccer skills at a very young age. He soon began putting them into practice with the Ridgeway Rovers.

A Ridgeway Rover

David was seven years old when he began playing for the Ridgeway Rovers in the Enfield District League. The fleet-footed youth with soccer abilities far beyond those of other boys his age soon became a star. He was the team's most talented scorer and tallied more than 100 goals by the time he was ten. His father, along with coaches Stuart Underwood and Steve Kirby, trained him. Beckham has never forgotten how much his days as a Rover

A Young Boy's Dream

David Beckham admits that he wanted to be a professional soccer player from a very young age:

"Mum, mum," I said, pulling at her skirt. At first she ignored me, but I persevered. "Mum!" Finally she looked down, wondering what all the fuss was about. "Mum, I'm going to be the captain of England [England's national soccer team] when I grow up." Don't ask me at what age I realized I wanted to be a professional soccer player. I've asked my parents and even they don't recall how old I was when I started telling everyone that I was going to play the game for a living. I think it's always been there. All I ever wanted to do was to play soccer and play it for Manchester United and my country. When I bothered my mum as a young boy, she would give me a knowing look as if to say, "That's nice, David, now go and play."

David Beckham, *David Beckham's Soccer Skills*. New York: HarperCollins, 2006, p. 22.

meant to him, not even after having played for two of the world's most famous teams and his country's national squad. When asked in an interview how good a team Ridgeway had been, the soccer star responded playfully:

The best! They'd beat Real Madrid, Manchester United, and England all together. Nah, I'm joking, but that was a massive part of my life, the first team I was involved with. I had a amazing time. Stuart Underwood was like a sergeant major. He scared me. In fact, I've always had managers and coaches that scared me.[14]

The budding young star joined the team the first season it started. His talent helped make the youth team successful even though he was not very big. Beckham admits that his lack of size in a sport that is very physical caused him problems when he was younger: "Because I was smaller than most, I used to get my share of knocks."[15] David made up for his small stature with speed, superior ball-handling skills, and physical endurance that allowed him to run hard for an entire game.

The Rovers became so successful that they began traveling to countries like Holland and Germany to play games. Underwood made the youngsters wear ties and jackets on such trips and imposed other strict rules on how the players had to behave when they traveled. Beckham has written that he liked being treated that way when he was young because "It made us feel special, but above all we felt professional."[16] When David was thirteen, he made his first visit to the United States to play in the Dallas Cup, a youth tournament in Texas.

David loved soccer so much that he also played pick-up games with friends and began attending soccer camps to improve his skills. It was at one of those training camps that he first became well-known as a player.

"A Great Experience"

The best soccer camps were run by professional teams or former players. The first one David attended was put on by London's Tottenham Hotspurs and in 1985 he went to Bobby Charlton's Soccer School in Manchester. He had learned about the camp while watching *Blue Peter*, a children's show.

Going to the camp was the most exciting thing that had ever happened to the young soccer player. For one thing, the week-long camp was conducted in Manchester, home to his beloved Red Devils. Secondly, it was run by Charlton, a Manchester United player who is one of the greatest of all English soccer players. In 1966 Charlton led England to the title in the World Cup, a competition every four years in which top teams from every country compete for soccer's world championship. David was homesick the first year he attended Charlton's school, and his play was also weakened by a toothache that slowed him down physically. He decided to return the next year to prove to Charlton that he was a better player than he had shown in the first camp.

Like other young children, David attended soccer camps run by professional teams and players (pictured here is Paul Scholes.)

He excelled during his second year by winning competitions on passing, shooting, dribbling, and other soccer skills that were held throughout the week. In addition, David won the overall competition for the week-long camp in his age group. The following December he and other weekly winners competed in the Bobby Charlton Soccer Schools National Skills Final. The event was held before forty thousand spectators at Old Trafford, United Manchester's stadium, before the Red Devils played the Hotspurs. Amazingly, the eleven-year-old triumphed over much older players. David's winning total in the various events was eleven hundred points, 150 more than sixteen-year-old runner-up Mark Price.

The legendary Charlton gave David a trophy for winning. The real prize, however, was a two-week training session in Spain run by Barcelona, one of Europe's top soccer teams. David went to Spain with Price; third-place runner-up Dean Lonsdale, thirteen; and a representative of Charlton's soccer school. Young athletes from other countries also attended the instructional camp. David loved training in Spain even though he was the youngest player and got some strange looks because of his youth, slight size, and strange hairstyle; he was cutting his hair in bristly spikes so he would resemble Manchester United's Gordon Strachan. "Everybody was really friendly but, at first, it was like: What's this child with the spiky hair and the funny [English] accent doing here?"[17] Although David seemed very young to the other players, most of them were between sixteen and nineteen years old, and he reveled in the chance to compete against older players from several countries and improve his game.

Going to Spain, however, was not the most important thing David gained from winning the Bobby Charlton competition. He believes the biggest prize he got was the attention of Manchester United scouts:

> That was a great experience for me because I ended up winning it the second year I went. People started recognizing me and apparently Bobby Charlton gave my name to Man United for them to look at me.[18]

Manchester United Comes Calling

After David returned from Spain, a Manchester United scout showed up at a game he was playing for Waltham Forest, a district-wide team for players under twelve. Manchester scout Malcolm Fidgeon was so impressed with the way David played that he accompanied Beckham home and talked to his parents. He arranged to pick David up a few days later and take him to Manchester for the first of several tryouts to judge his potential as a professional soccer player.

More athletes turn professional at a younger age in Europe than they do in the United States, so it is not unusual for professional soccer teams to scout players who are only eleven. In fact, even though David would not be able to play professionally for several more years, Manchester United was not the first pro team to show some interest in him. The Hotspurs and several other

David was scouted by Manchester United when he was only eleven years old. The club talked with his parents (pictured here in 2002), provided tickets to his family, and allowed David to meet the players.

London-area clubs had already contacted him, and he had even worked out with some team members, but Manchester pursued him the hardest on the advice of Charlton, who was impressed at the way David had played at his soccer camp.

Manchester United courted the talented young boy by providing his family tickets to games and allowing him to meet players and even eat meals with them. In 1986 the club made him the team mascot for a game against West Ham United. He dressed up in an official Manchester tracksuit and warmed up before the game with Strachan and other players including David Robson, his all-time hero. "They even let me sit on the bench for the game," Beckham remembered as an adult. "I even spotted myself on *Match of the Day* [a television soccer show] that evening."[19] David soon began to believe that he would one day be able to play for his beloved Manchester United.

David's Other Interests

Even though Beckham's early years were centered around soccer, he had other childhood interests. David's closest friend when he was young was a boy named John Brown who lived near his home. John did not like soccer, so the two friends spent time playing with Legos and later, as they got older, video games. David also engaged in other nonsoccer events with his friends—they rode their bicycles, roller-skated, played basketball, attended Boy Scout camp, and went to many movies.

When David got older and attended Chingford High School, he sang with the school choir, swam competitively, and ran cross-country. He even took Home Economics, partly because it was easier than a science class that was his only other alternative. David also took the class because he liked cooking. He became so proficient at cooking that when he was thirteen, he sometimes made dinner for his family when his mother was going to be home late from work. His favorite subject in school was art because he liked to draw, especially Walt Disney cartoon characters like Donald Duck. David also had two dogs, rottweilers which he named Puff and Snoop after the famous rap stars.

An Ancient Sport

Soccer, which is known in most countries as football, originated in England. It began in 1863 when the Football Association separated from rugby, another style of football, and began developing the sport. However, historian Wilfried Gerhardt writes that many games involving kicking a ball have been played for nearly a thousand years in Asia and Europe. The earliest known game was played in China during the second century B.C.:

> A military manual dating from the period of the Han Dynasty includes among the physical education exercises, the "Tsu'Chu." This consisted of kicking a leather ball filled with feathers and hair through an opening, measuring only 30–40 centimeters in width, into a small net fixed onto long bamboo canes—a feat which obviously demanded great skill and excellent technique. A variation of this exercise also existed, whereby the player was not permitted to aim at his target unimpeded, but had to use his feet, chest, back and shoulders whilst trying to withstand the attacks of his opponents. Use of the hands was not permitted. The ball artistry of today's top players is therefore not quite as new as some people may assume.

Wilfried Gerhardt, "History of the Game," International Federation of Football Association. www.access.fifa.com/en/history/history/0,3504,1,00.html.

David also loved to skateboard. Even though his parents did not want him to skateboard, he sometimes sneaked away to a nearby park that had a skating ramp. He once explained in an interview why his parents made him quit:

Another obsession of mine was skateboarding. All my friends would go over to the park and be on their skateboards having a brilliant time. I was banned from the ramps because

As a child, David had other interests besides soccer. One of his interests was skateboarding and he would sneak out to a skating ramp with his friends.

my mum got tired of me coming home with all sorts of bumps and bruises.[20]

Even though David sometimes defied his parents to go skateboarding, his father has said that David was always a good son. David also tried to be a good brother to his sisters Lynne and Joanne even though they sometimes resented him because of the attention he received. "They used to accuse us of spoiling David and, to a certain extent, I think they were right," Ted Beckham said.[21]

The Joy of Soccer

The young soccer player got that special treatment because he was so talented. But because his father made him realize that talent alone was not enough to become a professional soccer player, David worked very hard for many years to realize that dream. The many weary hours the young boy devoted to practicing and playing soccer, however, were nothing less than sheer delight because he loved the game so much. This is how Beckham describes the joy soccer gave him as a child:

> When I was eight years old, it was rare to find me doing anything other than playing soccer. All I needed was a ball and some space. Friends would join in, but if none were around, that was no problem—I would play alone. It was as simple as that. A park, a street, my yard, a playground, a field: these were all places where I could play the game that I had grown to love. The game I knew I would play when I grew up.[22]

Chapter 2

A Teenager Becomes a Professional Player

Even after David Beckham's brilliant showing at the Bobby Charlton Soccer School attracted the attention of Manchester United, there was no guarantee the eleven-year-old would ever play professional soccer. Beckham was supremely talented for someone his age, but young athletes in many sports often fail to fulfill such promise as adults. This usually happens because they lose interest in sports, are injured, or fail to develop the speed, strength, or other physical gifts they need to play at the pro level. It is always hard to predict whether a young athlete will one day become a professional. But when Bobby Charlton first saw Beckham play, he knew the young boy would one day be a soccer star:

> It's very difficult, actually, to pick out a youngster at that age [as a future pro], it's an art. It was an art that I have no gift for. But when I saw David Beckham, it was quite obvious that he was going to make it. He was just a natural. I didn't have to be a brain surgeon to see that.[23]

Charlton was not the only one who believed Beckham had a bright future. And for the next few years, several teams courted the young player in hopes of signing him when he was old enough play professionally.

A Player in Demand

Leytonstone Orient and Tottenham, two London area clubs, vied with Manchester United for the teen sensation. The teams gave Beckham and his family game tickets, let him meet players, and invited him to soccer camps they operated. Beckham enjoyed the attention and gifts from the London teams but never lost his original love for Manchester United. In fact, when Beckham attended

David attended training camps with several clubs before he signed schoolboy forms with Manchester United when he was fourteen years old.

one Tottenham training camp, he wore a Red Devils shirt even though Manchester was a Tottenham rival.

The first step toward becoming a professional player in the English soccer system is to sign schoolboy forms. Although U.S. professional teams rarely contact athletes in their early teens, European teams start recruiting them when they are teenagers. The schoolboy forms tie players to a club until they are sixteen, when they can sign a Youth Training Scheme (YTS) contract. A YTS is similar to an apprenticeship program for other jobs, and it allows teens to train with professional clubs.

Tottenham offered Beckham schoolboy forms when he was fourteen and promised to sign him to a YTS two years later. But when Manchester United offered similar terms, he chose the Red Devils because he had always loved the team. The teen made the formal commitment to Manchester on his fourteenth birthday in 1989. His father said that "David signing for Manchester United remains the proudest moment of my life."[24] Local newspapers ran stories about Beckham and he was interviewed on television. The ecstatic teenager told one TV reporter that "It was brilliant signing that paper. I couldn't believe it was happening."[25]

Beckham could have moved to Manchester to train with United coaches but decided to stay in Chingford and finish school. That two-year period would be the last in which Beckham lived an ordinary lifestyle.

Beckham Prepares for Manchester

Soccer remained Beckham's driving passion and he continued playing for the Brimstone (formerly Ridgeway) Rovers and other amateur teams. He also went to Manchester on school vacations for concentrated training sessions with other young recruits. Training camps during the summer were six weeks long. Beckham loved those extended stays in Manchester when he could learn soccer from former greats like Nobby Stiles, a youth coach who had played for Manchester as well as on England's World Cup champion team. Beckham writes that "the summers

During school vacations and summer break, David attended training camps in Manchester.

were fantastic" because he loved immersing himself in the sport with about thirty other young prospects:

> The soccer was what mattered above everything and it was a new experience, training day in day out and being introduced to more technical coaching. All the time I was at Ridgeway, I'd tried to imagine what it would be like and this was it: soccer was my job.[26]

In between the training sessions in Manchester, Beckham continued going to school in Chingford. As he got older, Beckham began to work at part-time jobs so he could earn some money. One job was a busboy in a restaurant at Walthamstow Stadium, a greyhound racing track. In a letter to a friend in 1991, Beckham bragged about how much money he had made: "I got my first wage packet [check] the other day and a bonus which come to 120 pounds [$220] so that went in my bank and I have got about 250 pounds [$450] in there now." But Val Yerral, who had hired him, said Beckham was a halfhearted worker because he was preoccupied with soccer. Said Yerral:

> His mind was never on the job he should've been doing, which was picking up the glasses. I would say, "C'mon, pick up some glasses!" Then I would say, "What are you talking about?" And he'd say, "Football." He was always on about football.[27]

Soccer was always on Beckham's mind because it was what mattered to him the most. When Beckham turned sixteen, he signed the YTS contract with Manchester United. On July 8, 1991, the sixteen-year-old moved 200 miles (322km) north to Manchester to train full time with the team.

A Manchester Trainee

Leaving home was not easy for Beckham. He writes that "I was very nervous about what lay ahead of me. Being away for a week or a month is completely different to moving away from home for

Beckham Cleans the Showers

When David Beckham was in Manchester United's Youth Training System, he had to do odd jobs around the training camp. He describes one of them :

> Like all young players, we had our jobs to do around the training ground. I remember Cas [Chris Casper] and I being put on the first-team dressing room, which meant we had to scrub the baths and showers and clean the dressing room itself. I got in there first and got the easy half of it: got my shorts on and just splashed around till the baths and showers were hosed down. Cas was too slow off the mark and got left with the mud and rubbish in the dressing rooms. We had a bit of a row [fight] about that one, and almost "got the ring out," which was when we'd wrap towels around our hands and have mock boxing matches to sort out an argument. To make matters even worse for him, we swapped jobs around Christmas. That meant I was assigned to the dressing rooms, looking busy cleaning boots, and ready to pick up the bonuses from the senior players at just the right time.

David Beckham with Tom Watt, *Both Feet on the Ground: An Autobiography*. New York: HarperCollins, 2004, p. 49.

good."[28] But his parents visited often and he made friends with other members of Manchester's youth team. His new teammates included future pro stars like Robbie Savage, Ryan Giggs, Gary and Phil Neville, Nicky Butt, and Paul Scholes. They trained, played, and even lived together; the team placed them in the homes of local families because they were too young to live on their own.

Beckham was generally well liked by his teammates. But Savage remembers that some Manchester-area players made fun of Beckham's working class London accent because it sounded strange to them. "He's got a shy little voice," Savage said of Beckham, who is soft-spoken, "and he got a lot of [teasing] about his accent. He used to just shake it off and go and practice free kicks against the wall for two hours."[29]

The urge to practice constantly had been drilled into Beckham by his father, who had told him over and over that he needed to work hard to be successful. That trait helped Beckham keep improving so that he could become a pro player. Charlton once said that Beckham's fierce desire to excel was as important to his success as his natural talent:

Beckham is unusual. He was desperate to be a footballer. His mind was made up when he was nine or ten. Many kids think that it's beyond them. But you can't succeed without practicing at any sport.[30]

Beckham soon became one of Manchester's top trainees and in his first season helped the team win the Milk Cup, a tournament in Coleraine, Ireland, that attracted teams of young players from many countries. It was the first of many titles Beckham would help Manchester United win.

Beckham Becomes a Professional

In Beckham's second season, his team won an even more prestigious event in May 1992—the Football Association (FA) Youth Challenge Cup for English players under eighteen. Manchester United defeated Crystal Palace by a combined score of 6–3 in a two-game series. It was Manchester's first Youth Cup since 1964, when legendary star George Best was on its youth team. Beckham had a goal in the first game, a 3–1 victory.

Although Beckham played mainly for the youth team that season, he made his debut on the regular Manchester squad on September 23, 1992, in a 0–0 tie against Brighton and Hove Albion. Beckham exploded with joy when a coach told him to enter the game as a substitute: "I was so excited, I jumped off the bench and cracked my head on the roof of the dugout: a great

Beckham scored his first Premier goal in a game against Aston Villa on August 19, 1995.

start to a first-team career."[31] His parents were equally thrilled to watch him play for seventeen minutes.

Beckham's promotion was brief and he was soon back with the youth team. However, he showed enough talent that season for United to offer him a professional contract, which the seventeen-year-old signed on January 22, 1993. He made several senior team appearances the next season on a United team that played in the Champions League. Beckham scored his first professional goal on December 7, 1994, in a 4–0 Champions League win over Galatasaray. English professional soccer has over 140 different leagues which are arranged in a descending order by skill level. The top division is the Premier League, which consists of twenty teams like Manchester United. The Champions League is in the second tier of pro teams.

In February 1995 Manchester United, believing Beckham needed more playing time to improve, loaned him for a month to Preston North End. Paul Mariner was a Preston assistant coach when Beckham arrived in early 1995. In only five games, Beckham scored two goals. The young player impressed Mariner:

> Natural. Natural. [He] had a lot of natural talent. The quality was there for all to see. Just his ability on the ball—miles ahead technically of the other players on the club. Just his vision, first touch, everything that you see now. He's just taken it to a higher level.[32]

Beckham was depressed to be loaned to Preston, which played in a lower-level league than Manchester United. But he performed so well that Manchester recalled him after a month and he became a first-team regular for good. He made his debut in the Premier League—England's top professional conference—on April 2, 1995, against Leeds United and on August 19 he scored his first Premier goal in a 3–1 loss to Aston Villa.

United had many young talented players like Beckham, but after that opening loss of the 1995–1996 season, soccer analyst Alan Hansen predicted that "You'll win nothing with kids."[33] The youngsters surprised Hansen and the rest of the league by winning their next five games and finishing first that season in the twenty-team league. That season they also captured the

FA Cup, an elimination tournament involving hundreds of English teams from every level of soccer.

Life was also good for Beckham off the field. During the season, he bought a three-story town house in Worsley, a community near Manchester. Beckham's working-class parents had provided Beckham and his two sisters with a decent home. Now the young soccer star was able to afford a much bigger place just for himself, one that cost about $500,000. Beckham describes how excited he was about the first home he owned:

> I'd grown up [in] a house just about big enough for the five of us. Now here I was, collecting the keys to a proper bachelor pad and making it my own: a den with a pool table, a leather suite in the front room, a Bang & Olufsen television and music system, and a great big fireplace. [There was] a cabinet at the bottom of my bed. You pressed a button and the television would come out of it.[34]

Beckham owed such luxury to his soccer prowess. He continued to display that talent the following year.

Beckham Becomes a Star

In the 1996–1997 season, Beckham helped United win another Premier League championship, playing so well that he was voted the league's Young Player of the Year. Beckham also started to become famous because of a dramatic goal he scored on August 17, 1996, in the first game of the season against Wimbledon. After taking a pass from Brian McClair, Beckham kicked the ball from the halfway line, which is 60 yards (55m) from the goal. The powerful kick floated the entire way and miraculously curved by Wimbledon goalie Neil Sullivan for a score.

The stunning shot, nicknamed the Wonder Lob, is considered one of the greatest in soccer history and brought Beckham overnight fame. As Beckham freely admits, that one shot changed his life: "Hardly anything—for better for worse—has been the same since."[35] It was such an amazing feat that Beckham was compared to Pele, the greatest soccer player ever. Beckham became

Beckham's famous kick from the halfway line, called the Wonder Lob, brought comparisons to soccer great Pele (right).

internationally known because he could bend or curve the ball more sharply and accurately than anyone else when he kicked it. This ability made him deadly in scoring goals because he could maneuver the ball over and past defenders into the goal.

World Cup Glory and Agony

The Wonder Lob also caught the attention of Glenn Hoddle, who coached England's national team in international competition. Hoddle, a player who Beckham admired while growing up, soon selected him to play against Moldova. On September 1, 1996,

The Wonder Lob

David Beckham owes much of his early fame to the Wonder Lob, the goal he scored on August 17, 1996, against Wimbledon. The shot was incredibly long—he was 60 yards (55m) from the goal when he kicked the ball—and the way it curved into the net seemed miraculous to thousands of fans watching and even players on both teams; even Wimbledon fans erupted in cheers, shouts, and loud applause. Beckham admits the loud celebration of his famous goal overwhelmed him:

> I hit it and it wasn't going straight for the goal at first and then it started to bend. And once it went in it was sort of weird because the whole place went silent and then there was this roar. The people just couldn't believe it and I just couldn't believe it. It was one of those things where it was quite surreal. The goalkeeper leaped but failed [to block the shot]. It was quite amazing for me to see the [frenzied] reaction of people, even the manager [United's Alex Ferguson] and teammates [were celebrating].

Really Bend It Like Beckham: David Beckham's Soccer Skills. Burbank, CA: Capital Entertainment Enterprise, 2005. 2 videodiscs (170 minutes).

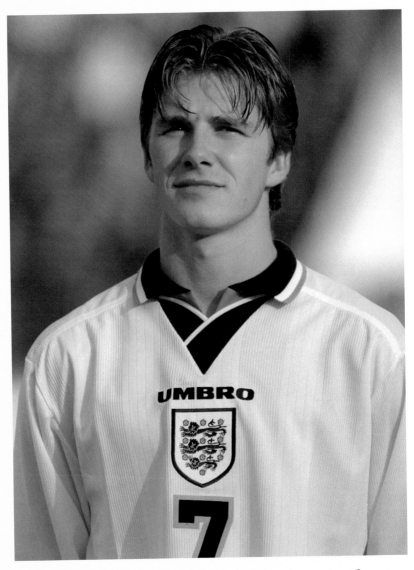

Beckham was selected to play for England's national team and he represented his team for the first time in 1996 during a game against Moldova.

in Kishinev, Moldova, Beckham was thrilled to represent his country for the first time. Beckham would later play in more than 100 games for England but has said the first time was the best: "Pulling on that England jersey remains a huge honor however many times you do it, but that first time is like a dream."[36] England won the game 3–0 and Beckham assisted on the opening goal.

The contest was one of a series of games countries were playing to qualify for the World Cup, which is held every four years and is soccer's premier tournament. Beckham played for England in every qualifying game leading up to the 1998 World Cup in France. Although Beckham was still playing full time for Manchester United, he relished the extra work because he loved representing his country. Beckham scored his first World Cup goal on June 26, 1998, against Colombia. It came on another amazing long-range kick in a game England won 2–0. The goal made Beckham a hero throughout England, but his image would soon be tarnished by an incident that would be the most damaging of his career.

England and Argentina have long had one of soccer's fiercest rivalries. The two teams met on June 30, 1998, in a World Cup game in Saint-Etienne, France. England and Argentina were tied 2–2 after the first half. In the opening minutes of the second period, Diego Simeone ran into Beckham, knocking him down. As Simeone was getting up, he playfully pulled Beckham's hair. Beckham, who was laying face down, responded angrily by kicking backward at Simeone. Although Beckham's foot barely grazed the Argentine player, Simeone fell down hard. Players sometimes fake reactions to slight touches to make officials call a foul on an opposing player, and Simeone's ploy worked. Beckham received a red card—the most severe penalty a player can get—for violent conduct and was ordered to leave the game. Simeone, who had actually knocked Beckham down, received only a yellow card, which was a warning, and he continued playing.

Beckham's absence left the English squad with only ten players. England fought hard and bravely and kept the game tied despite the one-man disadvantage until the end of regulation, when it lost anyway on penalty kicks, which are used to decide tie games. English fans blamed Beckham for the loss and the team's failure to advance to the World Cup finals. For one thing, Beckham's absence had weakened the English team during regulation play. And because Beckham was one of the greatest penalty kickers

"The Worst Night of My Life"

On June 30, 1998, Argentina defeated England in a World Cup game in Saint-Etienne, France. David Beckham was blamed for the loss because he was ejected from the game after kicking a player. Beckham describes what happened:

The match was perfectly poised, but then, just minutes into the second half, came the infamous moment that would propel me to become the nation's public enemy number one. The Argentine midfielder, Diego Simeone, clattered into me from behind. As I lay on the floor, he pretended to ruffle my hair but instead pulled it and I lashed out, kicking him in the back of the leg. He of course dropped like a sack of potatoes and that was that: I was [sent] off. I had retaliated and had to learn the hard way that you simply cannot do that and hope to stay in the game. It was horrible. The sixty seconds from being shown the red card to walking off past my aggrieved [angry] looking manager and down the tunnel will always remain with me. I can safely say that was the worst night of my life.

David Beckham, *David Beckham's Soccer Skills*. New York: HarperCollins, 2006, pp. 85–86.

of all time, they believed he could have helped England win in overtime. Not surprisingly, Beckham was as angry at himself as soccer fans were:

I stood in the tunnel and watched the last few minutes and the terrible tension of the penalty shoot-out. That was worse than anything else. It was then I fully realised what I had done. I kept thinking to myself that, if I had been out there,

I would have been one of the penalty takers. The rest of them had done so much without me and I had let them down desperately.[37]

Hated in England

The outburst of temper meant that Beckham, in a split second, went from being one of his country's most beloved sports heroes to a villain soccer fans hated. The anger the English felt was displayed the next day in headlines about the incident bannered in London newspapers—the *Times* called Beckham "a spoiled brat," the *Daily Mirror* declared "10 HEROIC LIONS, ONE STUPID BOY," and the *Daily Star* headlined "WHAT AN IDIOT."[38] Although thousands of soccer fans reacted emotionally to the defeat by turning against their one-time hero, many people believed that Beckham should not have been blamed for the loss.

In a newspaper interview, Glenn Hoddle begged of irate fans "Don't destroy him. We must not make Beckham the scapegoat for what has happened." The English coach said fans should not be angry at Beckham because he believed the referee in the game had unfairly ejected Beckham: "What David did, it shouldn't have been a red card. It wasn't violent conduct, which warrants an instant red. But even with 10 men I still thought we'd get through."[39] And teammate Teddy Sheringham went even further, accusing Simeone of shamelessly faking the foul:

> Becks should only have got a yellow card for that mistake. Oh yes, and there was Simeone's disgraceful reaction. If he has children I just hope one of them says: "Daddy, were you hurt when that England player touched you with his boot?" When he replies: "No," I just hope one of them asks him: "Well, daddy, isn't that cheating?"[40]

The incident marked the low point of Beckham's career. "I can safely say that was the worst night of my life," he has said.[41] But, amazingly, within a year Beckham would become more beloved than ever by English soccer fans.

Chapter 3

Beckham Achieves Worldwide Stardom

When David Beckham trotted onto the field for a game against Arsenal, the crowd of sixty-six thousand greeted him noisily. Instead of the cheers to which the player nicknamed "Becks" was accustomed, however, the fans were booing, taunting, and even cursing him. It was Manchester United's first game of the 1998–1999 season and the date was August 9, a little more than two months after England had lost to Argentina in the World Cup. The fans were still angry at Beckham because they believed his penalty against Diego Simeone on June 30 had cost England a chance to beat Argentina and win soccer's most coveted championship.

The game was held in Arsenal's stadium in Wembley, and Arsenal fans would have normally booed Beckham anyway because he was playing against their team. But the verbal abuse from tens of thousands of angry people was so stinging that one story about the game in an English newspaper was topped by a headline that read, "Becks' hate campaign starts here." Even Arsenal manager Arsene Wenger felt sorry for him, saying, "I hope people will soon forget and forgive because I think it is too easy to blame David Beckham for England's World Cup exit."[42] But even though Wenger did not believe Beckham deserved such treatment, he said Beckham had to be prepared for similar hostile receptions the rest of the season.

Manchester lost its opener 3–0. But even though Beckham had been booed and heckled every time he touched the ball, he was not very upset. That was because many worse things had happened to

Beckham, his family, and his fiancée—singer Victoria Adams of the Spice Girls—since his disastrous foul against Argentina.

England's Most Hated Man

Beckham's ejection from the game against Argentina ignited one of the most vicious backlashes any athlete has ever experienced because of something he or she did during a game. Furious English

Ted Beckham Fights for His Son

During the 1998–1999 season, David Beckham was able to ignore boos and verbal taunts from angry fans. Ted Beckham, his father, had more trouble doing that. In 1999 Beckham fought a Leicester City fan who was shouting negative comments at his son and other Red Devils while their team bus was driving away after a game. In a newspaper interview, Beckham explains how he confronted the man and they started fighting:

> I laid into him and we started brawling in the car park, trading blows in full view of the players. I was dimly aware of them [Manchester players] all crowding round to look out of the window while me and this bloke [man] were going for each other. [When the fight ended and] I was dusting myself down, my phone went [off]. It was David. "Did you hit him, Dad?" "Yes, I gave him a whack." David whooped with delight and shouted out, "He's hit him, lads, he's hit him." I heard the cheer in the background as the news spread through the coach.

Stephen Moyes and Fiona Cummins, "Exclusive: My David by Ted Beckham," *Daily Mirror* (London), September 20, 2005, p. 12.

Beckham's red card ejection from the game against Argentina created a huge backlash against the soccer star and his family.

fans bombarded newspapers and radio talk shows with negative, often obscene comments about Beckham's furious response to Simeone's rough play. Angry fans also attacked members of his family and Adams. The venomous outpouring of hatred angered Beckham because it hurt people he loved: "My mum, dad, nan [grandmother], and granddad were reading and seeing things that upset them, and that was the most upsetting part for me."[43]

There was a violent tone to much of the ill-feeling against Beckham. Fans put his picture on dartboards so they could riddle his image with pin holes. They also hung effigies or crude figures of him outside pubs where they drank and set them on fire. Some people sent Beckham, Adams, and his parents hate mail, and a few even threatened to harm them. After his parents' home was vandalized, Beckham hired a private security firm to protect his mother and father.

The most frightening threats came from the Inter City Firm (ICF), a group of soccer hooligans, a term for fans who engage in violent behavior at games. Colin Evans, who headed the security firm Beckham employed, said the group was bragging it would harm the soccer star: "The ICF have been telling people in pubs they are going to hurt Beckham."[44] The threats and nasty comments sickened Ted Beckham. In July he told a newspaper that "I'm no longer proud to be British after what they've done to my son. I'm disgusted with what has gone on. I've had enough."[45] He even said his son might leave England and play soccer somewhere else.

Beckham, however, was not going to let angry fans drive him out of his homeland. Instead, Beckham resolved to show them they were wrong and that he was a great player. Beckham explains how he made that decision:

> When people say the sort of things they were saying about me, you can either go home and cry, which I felt like doing because it was upsetting, or you come out fighting. Fortunately, I had people around me who made me come out and fight."[46]

The most important person who helped him was Adams, the singer known as Posh Spice who would soon become his wife.

Becks and Posh

Beckham and Adams had begun dating in the summer of 1997 after meeting when she and another Spice Girl made an appearance at a Manchester United game. Beckham said that Adams, who was then more famous than he was, had always been his favorite Spice Girl. He used the opportunity to get Victoria's telephone number and he called her to go out. They liked each other immediately and started dating.

Their relationship soon came to the attention of the English news media, which dubbed the celebrity couple "Posh and Becks" and reported on them constantly; photographers even camped outside his home hoping to snap a picture of them.

David Beckham and Victoria Adams pose after the announcement of their engagement. The press has dubbed them "Posh and Becks".

Beckham's courtship of Adams was often long distance because she was touring with the Spice Girls. He made up for not being with her by sending flowers to her at every hotel she stayed in. Beckham had had other girlfriends, but Adams was different. "As soon as I met Victoria," he writes, "I knew I wanted to marry her, to have children, to be together always."[47] Beckham proposed to her on January 24, 1998, and they began planning their wedding.

The Spice Girls had been performing in New York when Argentina defeated England in the World Cup. The next day, Beckham flew to New York to be with Victoria. Beckham has said that being with someone who loved him and believed in him helped him weather the controversy that was beginning to erupt over his penalty: "There is no way I would have survived the World Cup without Victoria. She didn't say anything, just gave me a big cuddle. Once I was with her I knew I would get through it."[48]

Their reunion was emotional for another reason besides his World Cup disappointment. Adams had called him shortly after the English team had arrived in Saint-Etienne for the World Cup game against Argentina to give him some startling news—she was pregnant. Beckham got the news while being bused from the airport to the hotel. He writes that he was so overjoyed that "I went into the tiny toilet on the coach and just jumped up and down, hugging myself. I was so happy."[49] Beckham did not tell anyone, however, because the news could be a distraction before the big game.

Beckham had a joyous vacation with Adams until July 13. On that day he flew home to begin training for Manchester United's upcoming season and to meet head-on the many soccer fans who now hated him.

"More Dangerous than Ever"

When Beckham got off the plane in London, he was greeted by a police escort because of the threats against him. He had learned what was happening in England by reading newspapers

Beckham scored the equalizing goal during Manchester United's Premier League season-opener against Leicester City.

and talking to family and friends, but the full impact of the wave of anti-Beckham feeling that had engulfed his country had not hit him until then. One of his first actions upon returning home was to apologize to fans for his mistake. Beckham issued a statement that included this line: "I will always regret my actions. I want every fan to know how deeply sorry I am."[50] Beckham then began training hard for the 1998-1999 season to apologize in another way, by playing better than he ever had before.

People who blamed Beckham were planning to try to disrupt games by taunting and booing him. But teammate Teddy Sheringham believed Beckham was strong enough to ignore such antics. Sheringham even predicted that fans who gave Beckingham "stick"—English slang for verbal harassment—risked making him play even better:

> Last season his strength of character shone out when Chelsea fans gave him stick—he put two goals past them. That's how he reacts. I think this ridiculous frenzy about his sending off will make him more dangerous than ever.[51]

Beckham got a chance to prove Sheringham right when Manchester United opened its Premier League season on August 15, 1998, against Leicester City. Even though the Red Devils were playing at home, Beckham was booed harshly by many in the crowd of 55,052 at Old Trafford. Manchester fell behind 2–0 in the first half, but in the second half Beckham led a stirring comeback as Manchester rallied for a 2–2 tie. Beckham helped set up the first goal by Sheringham and scored the second goal on a 25-yard (23m) free kick. The shot was met by a thunderous ovation from Manchester fans, who began chanting "One David Beckham, there's only one David Beckham" to the melody of the song "Guantanamera." It was a song that would be sung many times in the years ahead by Beckham's fans.

His brilliant play in that half marked the beginning of his climb back to the status of an English sports hero. Beckham's success would continue and result in Manchester United's greatest season.

Beckham Redeems Himself

The 1998–1999 season was the one in which Manchester United did something no English soccer team ever had—it won the treble. "Treble" is a slang term for the word *triple*, and in English soccer it refers to winning three major championships in one season. The championships are in the Premier League; the Football Association (FA) Cup, an event open to every pro team in England; and the Union of European Football Associations (UEFA) Champions League, which is restricted to top European teams. The team's run to the three major titles was fueled by an

Manchester United made history when the team won the "treble" during the 1998-99 season. The three major championships include the Premier League, the Football Association (FA) Cup, and the Union of European Football Associations (UEFA) Champions League.

incredible winning streak of thirty-three games from December 1998 to May 1999.

Manchester had failed to win any championship the season before. When the Red Devils lost their season opener to Arsenal, the defending Premier champions, it looked like they might struggle again. But once the Premier League started, they quickly became a contender for the championship. Beckham had a great season with a career-high nine goals, but his club had many other stars like Teddy Sheringham, Ryan Giggs, Andy Cole, and Ole Gunnar Solskjaer, who scored an amazing four goals in an 8–1

From Villain to Hero

David Beckham's brilliant play during Manchester United's treble season made him a hero again to English soccer fans. After Manchester defeated Newcastle United 2–0 on May 22, 1999, to win the Football Association Cup, a London newspaper said that Beckham had done much to erase the stigma of his 1998 World Cup blunder:

> The most moving moment at Wembley on Saturday afternoon was provided by the sight of an exhausted, elated David Beckham walking alone towards the few thousand Magpie-shirted Newcastle United fans left [in the stadium], looking them in the eye and raising his arms above his head to applaud their presence [and they returned] his salute with an instinctive warmth. Less than a year ago, we were being told that Beckham was the most reviled and despised creature in England, his effigy [image] burnt outside a public house and his famous girlfriend [Victoria Adams] the subject of obscene taunts. On Saturday she sat in the VIP seats and watched as he blew her a kiss of triumph [after the victory].

Richard Williams, "Beckham's Example Shows the Way as Ferguson's Men Turn Their Attention to the European Cup Final," *Independent* (London), May 24, 1999, p. 1.

Beckham celebrates after the FA Cup Final match against Newcastle United.

victory over Nottingham Forest. The Premier League title was decided in the final game on May 15, 1999, when Manchester United defeated Tottenham 2–1. Beckham scored one goal in the first half as the teams tied 1–1 and Cole got the game winner in the second half.

The FA Cup was first played in 1872 and is the world's oldest soccer competition. The 1999 event was held from January to May, with Cup games being interspersed with Premier League contests. The FA Cup is hard to win because it involves hundreds of English teams, both professional and amateur and because one loss knocks a club out of the running. Manchester opened with a 3–1 win on January 3 over Middlesbrough. Beckham made only one goal in the tournament's eight games, but it came in the semi-final on April 14 when Manchester defeated hated rival Arsenal 2–1. In the title game May 22, Manchester downed Newcastle United 2–0.

It was the third time that United had won both the Premier League and FA Cup championships. But even greater glory await-ed as the Red Devils still had a chance to win an historic treble by capturing the UEFA Champions League title. Games in that tournament had been played concurrently with the Premier and FA Cup championships. Even though all the important contests in the spring of 1999 were physically and emotionally draining for the players, Beckham said no one wanted to rest:

> None of us wanted to miss a single game of it. We were on the kind of roll where you'd finish one game and the adrenaline kidded you into believing that you could play another one the following day, no matter how heavy your legs were.[52]

"Kings of Europe"

The UEFA Champions League pits Europe's top teams against each other. The 1999 event began with qualifying matches in August 1998 and ran through the title game May 26, 1999, just four days after Manchester had won the FA Cup. The title game

The Manchester United team celebrates after winning the UEFA Champions League match against Bayern Munich of Germany.

matched Manchester and Bayern Munich of Germany. The teams were so evenly matched that they had tied each other 2–2 and 1–1 in two previous games in the tournament.

Manchester had to play the title game without starters Roy Keane and Paul Schole, who were suspended because of fouls in the previous game. But the Red Devils played well and won the game 2–1 on goals by Sheringham and Solskjaer. Both goals came after Beckham had won possession of the ball from German players and began the scoring sequences by kicking the ball to a teammate. Beckham had played brilliantly throughout the season, especially because of the often-hostile reception he got from fans. After the game, however, he said the victory was won by everyone on the team:

> This victory wasn't just for the players on the pitch but for everyone involved in this great club. You could tell that at the end when [the manager] wanted Roy Keane out there holding the trophy. He might not have played but, believe

me, he was there in spirit. It's the same spirit between the players that's made us complete this wonderful Treble.[53]

The victory earned the Red Devils a new nickname, the "kings of Europe" because they reigned as soccer champions. But Beckham had played so well that he was individually honored by finishing second in voting to Vitor Borba Ferreria, who is nicknamed Rivaldo, for the 1999 European Footballer of the Year and Federation Internationale de Football Association (FIFA) World Player of the Year awards. Beckham continued his fine play over the next two years to help Manchester win the Premier title for three consecutive seasons.

World Cup Glory

Beckham's exceptional play for Manchester United made him a worldwide sports hero. Some English fans, however, still disliked him because of his World Cup blunder against Argentina, and they often heckled him mercilessly during games. But Beckham was so playing so well that he was chosen again and again for England's national team, and he soon began winning over even his fiercest World Cup critics with his fine play.

Beckham became such a strong force on the international squad that he was named the team's captain on November 15, 2000. Being captain had been one of his childhood goals, and he was delighted to captain England later that day against Italy: "Leading the team out against Italy—never mind it was an exhibition, never mind the stands weren't full—was one of the proudest moments of my whole life."[54]

England lost to Italy 1–0, but Beckham played well. He also became determined to help England win more games, especially in World Cup competition. He got his chance on October 6, 2001, in a game against Greece. England needed to win or tie the game to qualify for the 2002 World Cup. England was losing 2–1 late in the contest when Teddy Sheringham was fouled. Beckham was chosen to take the kick, and one of his signature curling kicks found its way into the goal to tie the game and send England to the World Cup tournament.

Beckham helped England qualify for the World Cup with his tying goal against Greece in 2001.

That kick led directly to Beckham's greatest World Cup moment, one that would finally redeem him with every English soccer fan who was still angry about his foul against Argentina in 1998. On June 7, 2002, England and Argentina faced each other again in Sapporo, Japan, in a second round World Cup game. Beckham scored the game's only goal on a penalty shot to defeat Argentina 1–0. Several years later, he explained how nervous he was before he took the shot:

I actually remember standing there and not being able to breath. I literally couldn't catch my breath because of the excitement and anxiety of what would be ahead of me. There's such a thin line between success and failure. If I would have missed that penalty, then what would people have said again. For me to score that was an amazing feeling.[55]

How to Survive Mistakes

David Beckham's mistake in the 1998 World Cup game against Argentina almost ruined his career. Beckham once told a group of youngsters that they have to learn how to deal with such mistakes if they want to be good players:

> As you all know, I made a mistake in the World Cup. I had to face all my teammates when I went into the changing room after that. But all my teammates were good to me. They talked to me, they said, "You know, it's not a problem." But mistakes happen in football. That's something that's part and parcel of being a footballer. The hardest thing is you have disappointments along the way. If you can get over them, that's the best way you can become a footballer. Sometimes you're disappointed in games and it gets you down. But you have to keep on thinking that you can be the best player in the world.

Really Bend It Like Beckham: David Beckham's Soccer Skills. Burbank, CA: Capital Entertainment Enterprise, 2005. 2 videodiscs (170 minutes).

England was knocked out of the tournament in the quarter-finals 2–1 by Brazil, which went on to win the cup. Beckham's heroics wiped away the bitterness he still felt over the 1998 game and finally made him a hero to every English soccer fan.

Adversity Made Beckham Strong

The four years in which Beckham was the target of irate soccer fans was one of the hardest periods of his life. Beckham was able to bear the taunts about himself, but he was hurt and angered by those aimed at his parents and other people he loved, like Adams. After her pregnancy was made public in 1998, some hecklers at games would loudly ask Beckham if he knew who the baby's father was. Such lewd comments continued even after Brooklyn Joseph Beckham was born on March 4, 1999, and the couple was married on July 4, 1999.

The abuse of his family hurt Beckham the most. But in a 2006 interview, he said that all the bad things he endured during that period actually helped him. Said Beckham:

> I look back on it and, of course, I wish it hadn't happened. But on the positive side I think if it hadn't happened, I might not be the person and I definitely wouldn't have been the player I am today because it taught me a big lesson about respect and it made me stronger.[56]

Chapter 4

Celebrity Royalty: "Posh and Becks"

When David Beckham visited Victoria Adams in New York City in July 1998, he was introduced to the celebrity lifestyle his future wife lived as a Spice Girl. Adams at the time was more well-known than Beckham and knew many famous people, including Madonna, who Beckham met before the Spice Girls performed at Madison Square Garden. Beckham has admitted he was stunned the singer knew who he was when she came backstage to greet the Spice Girls: "I just kept quiet and tried to make sure my mouth wasn't hanging open. Then she turned to me: 'Oh, you're the soccer player, aren't you?' How did Madonna know who I was? I was dumbstruck."[57]

Although Beckham was famous in England, he was only just becoming well-known in other countries. In the next decade, however, Beckham's fame exploded and many people believed he deserved the title of the world's most famous athlete. Even Tiger Woods, the golfer who was one of a handful of superstars who could rival Beckham's global popularity, believed that Beckham was more famous than he was. In August 2007 after an ESPN television poll selected Woods as the world's best-dressed athlete, Woods said, "I don't see how Beckham didn't beat me." Woods admitted Beckham should have won because more people around the world knew the soccer star:

> As far as global figures, he's probably far more global than
> I am. You know, golf is not truly played all around the world,

it is played in most places but not like soccer or football is. I think that [poll] was just about in America. If it had gone globally, it would have been probably different.[58]

Soccer's popularity is one of three other major factors that have made Beckham a global sports icon. The other two are that Beckham married another celebrity and that he has a personality and quirky lifestyle that appeal to many types of people other than sports fans.

England's Royal Couple

Beckham's fame increased greatly when he married Victoria Adams because she was known and beloved throughout the world as Posh Spice, a member of the Spice Girls, a hugely successful all-female musical group. Adams was born on April 17, 1974, near London. Although she grew up only a few miles away from Beckham, her life was much different because her family was richer; her father had a Rolls-Royce and other luxury cars, and she attended private schools. Like Beckham, she decided as a young child what she wanted to be—a famous singer. Adams said the idea began after her mother took her to a Barry Manilow concert:

> I sat there looking at the stage thinking: "I want to be up there." I used to dream that when I went shopping there would be books and pencils and pencil sharpeners with my name on [them]—I imagined things like that all the time.[59]

Adams began to get the fame she desired in 1994 when she became a member of Touch, an all-girl band in London that a year later changed its name to Spice Girls. The group's first popular song was "Wannabe" in July 1996. In the next few years, more hit records and successful tours in countries around the world made the Spice Girls famous. The members of the band—Adams, Melanie Brown, Emma Bunton, Melanie Chisholm, and Geri Halliwell—were also known by the nicknames Scary Spice, Baby Spice, Sporty Spice, and Ginger Spice. Adams was dubbed Posh

Spice because she dressed elegantly and her aloof, regal attitude made her seem high-class.

When Beckham and Adams began dating, their fame magnified. Sports fans who liked Beckham and music fans who loved the Spice Girls became interested in the other half of the famous couple. Their fame was spread by the news media, which constantly ran pictures and stories about "Posh and Becks," the media's nickname for the happy young couple. They became so popular that when they were married on July 4, 1999, in Lutrellstown Castle near Dublin, Ireland, the British magazine *OK!* paid 1 million pounds (more than $2 million) for the right

A Little Girl's Dream

When David Beckham started dating Victoria Adams, the singer known as Posh Spice, she was more famous than he was. They both became worldwide celebrities by realizing the dreams they had as children. Victoria explains how a television show she watched as a child and a teacher helped ignite her dream to be an entertainer:

> I loved a kids' show called *Emu's House* with Emu, Rod Hull, and big fat Grotbag. Every time a bell rang, a group of young stage school kids would come on dancing and singing. "That's the doorbell! That's the doorbell!" I'd sit there thinking: "I want to be one of those dancers." They looked really cool and wore bright shorts and bright tops and far too much makeup. . . . At junior high school my teacher, Mrs. Harvey, helped me get used to performing in front of audiences from an early age. No one ever did any work after lunch because she'd get me to do a dance on the carpet with everyone sitting there watching me.

The Spice Girls, *Real Life = Real Spice: The Official Story*. London, England: Azone/VCI, 1997, p. 31.

David Beckham and Victoria Adams became one of the most famous couples in the world after their marriage.

to take exclusive photographs. The wedding was attended by more than four hundred friends and family members, including celebrities like Elton John.

At the lavish wedding reception afterward, the Beckhams sat on red-velvet thrones; between them was Brooklyn, who was four months old. Beckham said they used thrones to have fun: "The whole thing was tongue-in-cheek [just for fun], of course: we were at a castle, weren't we? And the pair of us were Lord and Lady of the Manor for the day."[60] It is not unusual for English people to want to be considered royalty. In England Queen Elizabeth and other members of royal families are that country's most revered residents. In the next few years, the Beckhams achieved a level of fame and adulation that only royalty usually received. When they bought a $15-million, 25-acre (10ha) estate in 1999 in the countryside just outside London, the media nicknamed it "Beckingham Palace"; that was a pun on "Buckingham Palace," the queen's London residence.

Beckham's increasing celebrity status, however, was due to much more than who he married. In fact, as the couple had two more children—Romeo James on September 1, 2002, and Cruz David on February 20, 2005—and the Spice Girls quit performing, he became more famous than Victoria.

Beckham's Many Admirers

In May 2002 Beckham became the first man to appear on the cover of *Marie Claire*, a women's fashion magazine. Marie O'Riordan, the magazine's editor, said she chose Beckham because "he represents something for every woman—father, husband, footballer, icon. In a word, he's the ultimate hero."[61] *Marie Claire* printed up an extra sixty thousand copies of the magazine because it knew Beckham had so many female fans. Ironically, his wife had appeared on the magazine's cover a year earlier.

Part of Beckham's appeal to many of his fans, both men and women, is how he dresses. Even though Beckham once wore a sarong in public, he is noted for wearing expensive, stylish clothes and has been named to many best-dressed lists. His hairstyle has drawn even more attention because he keeps changing it. In addition to dying it different colors, Beckham has worn his hair down to his shoulders, braided it into plaits, cut it in a Mohawk, and buzzed it down to blond fuzz. Each new hairdo has been reported in the media, which sometimes criticize his styles. Beckham, however, claims he does not care what people think: "Me! There's none I regret because at the time I felt it looked good. Sometimes I'm bored of my hair so I cut it. Today it's long, tomorrow it could be short again."[62]

Beckham's sometimes bizarre hairstyles make him appealing to unconventional people who may not be sports fans. So do the dozen tattoos that adorn his body. The skin art includes the names of his three sons; "Victoria" spelled in Hindi; several Latin phrases, including *Perfectio In Spiritu*, which in English means "Spiritual Perfection"; and a winged cross on his neck. Beckham said he thinks carefully before getting a tattoo: "Each one has a meaning to my career or my life. I don't just go into a shop and pick one out. I have friends who do that, and they're always regretting it 10 years after."[63] Even though Beckham claims the

Beckham changes his hairstyles often, which has made him appealing to non-soccer fans.

four-by-six-inch cross he got in 2004 is a symbol of protection for his family, a London newspaper, the *Mirror*, ran a picture of the tattoo with a headline that said, "YUK! The new tattoo that makes Becks look like a hooligan [criminal]."

Another group of people who admire Beckham are homosexuals. Although some athletes are antigay, Beckham in 2002 posed for the cover of *Attitude*, an English gay magazine, He accepts gay people and defends their right to choose their own lifestyle. Claims Beckham:

> Being a gay icon is a great honor for me. I'm quite sure of my feminine side, and I've not got a problem with that at all. These days it's the norm, and it should be. Everyone's different, everyone's got their thing.[64]

Because Beckham appealed to so many different kinds of people, companies flocked to him to advertise their products. He began making millions of dollars a year to endorse things like Adidas soccer shoes and sportswear, Police Sunglasses, Pepsi soda, and Gillette razors and blades. His image appeared regularly in almost every country in the world, including Iran, a country that had banned such western ads since 1979 because Muslim religious leaders believed they were immoral.

Beckham's Celebrity Lifestyle

Incredible worldwide fame and the money it allows him to earn have given Beckham and his family the chance to live lavishly. They reside in luxurious homes which he has bought in several countries. The Beckhams live in "Beckingham Palace" when they are in England, and Beckham also purchased lavish estates in Spain and the United States when he played for teams there. Beckham has owned many expensive automobiles including a $220,000 Lamborghini Gallardo, a $120,000 Range Rover SUV with bulletproof doors, and a Rolls-Royce limousine. His wife, who is rich in her own right because of her days as a pop star, bought Beckham the Rolls for Christmas in 2005, the same year he gave her a ruby and diamond necklace worth $2.4 million.

Although Beckham still has friends from his childhood, he also knows and socializes with many celebrities like actor Tom Cruise and his wife, Katie Holmes. Although Beckham and his wife are unfazed to know such famous people, Ted Beckham is

The Beckhams have several homes in several different countries. While in England, they reside in what has been dubbed "Beckingham Palace".

amazed at some of his son's friends. He has said, "As for Tom Cruise, I can't believe they're friendly with one of the biggest stars in the world."[65] The Beckhams are so close to the famous actor that they named their third son—Cruz—after him. And when Brooklyn and Romeo were baptized, their godparents were two other famous entertainers, actress Elizabeth Hurley and singer Elton John.

Despite their celebrity lifestyle, the Beckhams try to raise their sons as normally as possible, including taking care of them directly

David Beckham as a Father

David Beckham likes to say "My kids are my life." But in an interview with the English newspaper *Mail on Sunday*, he explains that his love is tinged with discipline because he wants his sons Brooklyn, Romeo, and Cruz to grow up to be good people:

Discipline is very important to David Beckham.

> I am quite strict, believe it or not, in every way. For example, the only time my boys will leave their clothes on the floor is when they get in the bath and even then they aren't allowed in the bath until their clothes are in the laundry bin. . . . We have the naughty stair at home and if they have been naughty they sit on the second step of the stairs. If we're somewhere else, they'll sit on a naughty chair. I'm very strong on respect. I bring my sons up to show respect to people. [The boys] will never get anything unless they have said "Please" or "Thank you." I absolutely make sure of that, and so does Victoria.

Louise Gannon, "Becks to the Future," *Mail on Sunday* (London), February 26, 2006, p. 12.

without hiring nannies to do so. Beckham once explained that they do this so that their children will know and love them: "I picked up Brooklyn from school [one day], and this boy fell over in the playground. Instead of running to his mum, he ran to the nanny; that image always haunts me. I want my kids to know me."[66] He enjoys spending time with Brooklyn, Romeo, and Cruz, especially teaching them how to play soccer as his father did with him. And like dads everywhere, Beckham changed their diapers when they were infants.

Both Beckhams try to shield their children from the endless news media coverage that they attract on a daily basis. Victoria explains:

> We don't ever allow the children to be photographed or filmed. We like them to be normal kids. Anything we do professionally, we try to keep the children out of it. We don't sort of traipse them up and down the red carpet.[67]

But the riches that enable the Beckhams to live the way they do also has negative side effects. One of them is a threat to their safety.

Drawbacks to Celebrity

In November 2002 police in England arrested nine people for planning to kidnap Beckham's wife and sons so they could ransom them for more than $10 million. Victoria was frightened when police told her about the potential kidnapping: "It's clear these people were serious and that, of course, has scared the life out of me." Police alerted Victoria first. She waited until later the same day to tell David about the plot because he was playing a game for Manchester United. Beckham vowed to make sure nothing like that could ever happen because "the first role of a father and husband is to keep his family safe."[68]

Beckham had already hired bodyguards to protect his family because of previous reports of possible kidnappings and attempts to harm them. He had also installed surveillance cameras and other security measures at homes they owned, Beckingham Palace near London and another near Manchester he used to be close to his team. Beckham now increased those security measures to protect his family. He also purchased

Potential kidnappings, death threats, and the constant hovering of photographers are some of the drawbacks to Beckham's fame.

bulletproof vests for himself because of recent rumors that some people wanted to kill him. Beckham had actually lived with such threats for years. The first was in 1998 when someone sent him bullets with his name carved on them shortly after he began dating Victoria and there were more after the World Cup match against Argentina.

For Beckham, the fear that someone might harm his family was the most frightening aspect of becoming rich and famous. Beckham, like many other celebrities, admitted he never expected to have such problems because of his success: "I always dreamed of being a famous footballer, Victoria dreamed of being famous. Yet I don't think you actually realize what comes with that."[69]

The other major problem Beckham faced was the ceaseless media attention from photographers and journalists who followed him and his family everywhere and reported on everything they did. Beckham explained that he hated being spied on all the time while in public: "Is there any privacy for me? In my own home when the curtains are closed but apart from that that's it." The members of the media that anger celebrities the most are called paparazzi, a nickname for photographers who constantly hound celebrities to take their pictures. Beckham told about one incident in which he almost hit a photographer:

> I nearly lost it once. Me and Victoria were out having a meal and two photographers jumped out from nowhere and one of them knocked her with their camera. She was pregnant at the time, so I snapped at them, but these days, you can get sued for so many things, so I keep my temper in check.[70]

Beckham also hates some stories written about him and his family because a few journalists make up facts for stories or accept as truth anything that anybody tells them. "Every single day," Beckham once said, "people are making up things, lying."[71] Beckham said such false stories include one about his spending more than $50,000 to buy one of his sons an earring for his fifth birthday. Beckham has also denied reports that surfaced in 2004 that he had affairs with two women—Rebecca Loos and Sarah Marbeck—and criticized the media for attacking him. Beckham claimed that "the way I and my family have been treated is an absolute disgrace because at the end of the day I'm a nice person and loving husband and father."[72] However, the women stuck by their claims and Loos, who had been his personal assistant, got more than $2 million from a British television station for interviews about the alleged relationship.

The kind of fame that celebrities like Beckham have can cause problems in their personal lives. However, they can also use it to do many good things.

The Power of Celebrity

In 2003 Beckham received the ultimate compliment with the release of *Bend It Like Beckham*, a movie about two young English women who dreamed of playing soccer. Beckham was the hero

In 2004, Beckham was appointed a Goodwill Ambassador for UNICEF.

of one of the women, and in the movie a poster of Beckham taped to the ceiling of her bedroom helps inspire her to work hard to reach her goal. The poster is the only image of Beckham in the movie. Some sports stars might have sought money for use of their name for the movie's title, but Beckham allowed producers to use it for free because he knew the film would promote women's soccer.

Beckham has also helped raise money for many charities including the United Nations Children's Fund (UNICEF). He has had a long relationship with the charity which helps children around the world combat poverty, hunger, and disease. In 2006 Beckham and his wife raised several million for UNICEF by hosting a party prior to the World Cup. Beckham has done so much that in 2004 United Nations secretary-general Kofi Annan named him a goodwill ambassador for the group.

Like many famous people, Beckham has occasionally used his fame to help individuals like Rebecca Johnstone of Hamilton, Canada. She was a soccer player who idolized Beckham so much that her friends called her "Beccam"; they merely added m to her nickname of Becca. In January 2007 Beckham called her in an attempt to cheer her up when he learned that Johnstone was dying of cancer. The gravely ill young woman was shocked and delighted her hero had called, and they talked about soccer for several minutes. A few days later he sent her one of his jerseys, and on the back he had written "To Rebecca, With Love,

Selling Products

David Beckham's worldwide fame has helped sell many types of products from athletic shoes to shaving blades. When Beckham was in Madrid, Spain, July 1–2, 2003, to sign a contract to play for Real Madrid, he was driven around the city in Audi cars because the automaker was a sponsor of the team. News stories contained so many pictures of Audi cars that Jesus Gazanz, president of Audi in Spain, was ecstatic. He claimed it was the most powerful free advertising any company ever got because of the fame of one person:

> Such was the international media clamor for pictures of David Beckham that the Audi he traveled in was continually on TV and in newspaper photographs everywhere. I turned out to be the greatest news coverage in the world, in history I am sure, in which one company was visibly associated with the brand it sponsored. . . . Neither the pope nor the president of the Untied States, not anyone else I can think of, could give us publicity like that.

John Carlin, *White Angels: Beckham, Real Madrid and the New Football*. New York: Bloomsbury, 2004, p. 68.

David Beckham." Rebecca died not long afterward, but the call and present gave her immense joy in her final days of life. Bill Johnstone, a cousin, said, "It was something that was a lot larger than what anyone thought could happen."[73]

Beckham Likes Being Popular

The power to help people is one of the things Beckham likes about being a celebrity. And because Beckham is admired by so many different types of people, he believes that popularity can help to unite people who are dissimilar in a common bond. In an interview on May 2, 2003, his twenty-eighth birthday, Beckham said:

> I do like that. It's part of my personality and my life [that he appeals to different types of people]. I think it's important that people come together because there's too much going on in the world to worry about our differences.[74]

Beckham Stars in Spain and the United States

In 2000 Thongruang Haemhod, a sculptor who lives in Thailand, created a statue of David Beckham that was 1-foot (0.3m) high and covered with gold leaf. He placed it in the Pariwas Buddhist temple in Bangkok in an effort to keep the memory of his favorite player alive for a thousand years. Chan Theerapunyo,

A young boy studies the golden image of David Beckham in the Pariwas Buddhist temple in Bangkok. The statue was created by sculptor Thongruang Haemhod in 2000.

Beckham Almost Quits

David Beckham said once in a newspaper story that his feud with Alex Ferguson in 2003 nearly made him give up the sport he loves:

> It did get to the point where I wasn't considering playing anywhere else. I actually did discuss retiring with Victoria. [It] shocked her because she realized how serious I was about it. She realized there was a real problem there and that I really wasn't happy. I didn't want it to start affecting my family life and my children. She said, "I'll support you whatever you do." She was the one who sat down and said, "Things are not really that bad. You're going through a tough time at the moment, but look at the positives." She was the one who changed my mind and turned it all around for me. She said that I'd been given a great opportunity in life. She explained how important Man U [Manchester United] was to me and how important football is to so many people. It just turned me straight around. I just got on with things.

Ben Jackson, "Beckham: 'It Got So Bad I Was Ready to Quit Football,'" *Sun* (London), August 29, 2003, p. 1.

the temple's senior monk, explains why he allowed Beckham's image to be displayed at the foot of a towering Buddha along with other statues of people and religious dieties: "Football has become a religion and has millions of followers. So, to be up-to-date, we have to open our minds and share the feelings of millions of people who admire Beckham."[75]

Such global hero worship for Beckham was fueled by never-ending news media coverage and the fact that his face seemed to be everywhere on billboards and television and magazine advertisements. Even though Beckham helped make Manchester United the world's most popular soccer team, manager Alex Ferguson began to believe his growing fame and celebrity lifestyle were hurting his playing ability. In 2003 Ferguson claimed Beckham was no longer as focused on being a great player as he had been when he first joined the club:

> After training he'd always be practicing, practicing, practicing [but then] his life changed when he met his wife, really. She's in pop [music], and David got another image. And he's developed this fashion thing. I saw his transition to a different person.[76]

Ferguson's concerns about Beckham's lifestyle created tension between them. Their relationship deteriorated so much that Beckham began to wonder if he could continue playing for United.

"Fergie's Flying Boot"

The rift between Beckham and Ferguson deepened during the 2002–2003 season. An example of the ill will between them was a comment Ferguson made after he allowed Beckham to skip practice to care for an ill son. When Ferguson heard that Victoria had been out shopping that day, he angrily told Beckham: "You were baby-sitting while your wife was out gallivanting."[77] Beckham was hurt that Ferguson would criticize him for helping his son.

Their feud made front-page headlines following a locker-room incident on February 17, 2003. When Ferguson blamed Beckham's poor play for a 2–0 loss to Arsenal, Beckham began shouting back at him. Ferguson was so angry that he kicked a soccer shoe toward his star player; the shoe's cleats hit Beckham on the forehead, opening a cut that required several stitches to close. Several players then had to stop Beckham from attacking Ferguson. The manager tried to minimize the incident by claiming, "It happens every night in a dressing room."[78] But the story of "Fergie's flying boot" made soccer fans around the world realize the situation.

Ferguson began keeping Beckham out of the starting lineup even though he was still playing well. The most famous example

Beckham's rift with Manchester United coach Alex Ferguson deepened in 2003 when Ferguson began keeping Beckham out of starting lineups.

of this occurred on April 23, 2003, when United met Real Madrid. Real won the first game of the two-game series 3–1 in Bernabéu, their stadium in Spain, and the finale was played at Manchester. Beckham did not play until late in the game. But eight minutes after he trotted onto the field, Beckham scored one of his trademark long kicks to tie the game 3–3 and fourteen minutes later he made a short-range goal. Beckham's scores gave Manchester a 4–3 victory, but United lost the series 6–5.

Many people believed Manchester could have won the series if Beckham had played the entire game. One of them was

Madrid coach Vicente del Bosque, who said that "Had a Spanish coach done that in a game of that magnitude, he'd have been fired. No doubt about it."[79] But the legendary English coach was so powerful that he could do what he wanted, even to a star like Beckham.

From Manchester to Real Madrid

Although Beckham only talked about the situation to family members and close friends, he was miserable during this period. Beckham later admitted publicly that he was so upset he considered quitting soccer:

> I was in a place where I felt I couldn't control things. I'm never, ever like that. I'm always in control of what's going on around me and what's going on with my family. But I just felt that the only way out of this was to leave everything and not play football again. Because that was what was causing me to be unhappy.[80]

Beckham eventually decided he still wanted to play soccer but he knew he could not stay with Manchester. The unpleasant situation was resolved when United began trying to trade Beckham to other teams. Real Madrid expressed interest in Beckham, and the two teams started negotiating six days after their Champions League game in Manchester. To the anger of English soccer fans, United agreed to sell Beckham to Madrid for $50 million on June 17. Gordon Taylor, chief executive of England's Professional Footballers' Association, criticized the move by saying, "You wouldn't want to sell your second-hand car in such a way, never mind one of your finest assets."[81] Even though $50 million is a lot of money, many English soccer fans believed Beckham was worth even more.

Critics of the deal claimed that Manchester discarded Beckham because Ferguson was jealous of Beckham's fame and wealth. Beckham, however, has never condemned Ferguson for the trade. In an interview after the trade Beckham said,

In the summer of 2003, Manchester United sold Beckham to Real Madrid for $50 million.

"As much as we had our ups and downs, people have to remember he was a father figure to me for a long time and I'll always remember that."[82]

Beckham the Galactico

Beckham signed with Madrid on July 1, 2003. He would earn $7 million a year plus 50 percent of royalties on team merchandise bearing his name and jersey number (23). Despite the large salary, it was not easy for Beckham to decide to move to Spain. Beckham hated leaving England and was worried about how his wife and sons would adapt to life in a foreign country. But Victoria's support for the move made his decision easier, as did the fact that he wanted to play for Real Madrid. In an interview after signing his contract, Beckham said:

> This was the only team I wanted to come to. Real Madrid excited me. They're a great club, massive club, and this was the only team that actually excited me. They play amazing football, exciting football, but effective football as well.[83]

The irony of Beckham's departure from Manchester is that he had helped it win the Premier League title in his final season. Real Madrid wanted Beckham because it believed he could help it win championships In La Liga, the Spanish league. And the club had no concerns about Beckham's commitment to the game despite his celebrity lifestyle. Jorge Valdano, Real's sporting director, said,

Real Madrid had several superstar players and they were nicknamed the Galacticos. Pictured from left: Beckham, Luis Figo, Ronaldo, Zinedane Zidane, and Raul.

"The impression that he cares too much about his show-business life is wrong. Despite all the media pressure, he has the ability to concentrate on just his football."[84]

Beckham scored five goals in his first sixteen games, winning over Spanish fans but he was not Real's only superstar. The club already had world-class players in Zinedine Zidane, Ronaldo Luis Nazário de Lima, Roberto Carlos, and Luis Figo. Beckham and the others were nicknamed the Galacticos, a Spanish nickname for star players. Even though Beckham played well and was surrounded by so many other talented players, Real Madrid in the next few seasons won only the 2003 Spanish Super Cup, a minor championship. That was a comedown for a club that had won twenty-nine La Liga titles in the past.

Real Madrid did not get its elusive thirtieth La Liga until June 18, 2007, when it beat Mallorca 3–1 to finally capture that championship again. Beckham was hobbled by a left-ankle injury and failed to score, but he had played well in other games and was ecstatic with the championship: "I couldn't have dreamt it any better. It's been about winning the title for the last six months, and we've deserved it."[85]

In the game's final minutes, Beckham bent down and kissed the field. His emotional gesture was a dramatic good-bye to the stadium because it was his last game for Real Madrid. Beckham had already signed a contract to play for the Los Angeles Galaxy.

From Galactico to Galaxy

Real Madrid's lack of success in Beckham's four years with the team was due to a constant turnover of players and coaches. Faced with such turmoil, Beckham began considering offers from other teams, including the Galaxy of the Major League Soccer (MLS) in the United States. The Galaxy wanted Beckham because it believed the world's most famous player could help boost the image of soccer in the United States, where sports like baseball, football, and basketball were all more popular. Beckham liked the challenge of trying to boost the image of the sport he loved to play in the world's richest nation.

Despite his anger at Beckham's contract with the L.A. Galaxy, Real Madrid's new coach, Fabio Capello, believed that Beckham was the key to winning the La Liga championship.

Beckham signed a contract in January 2007 that would give him an average salary for five years of about $10 million. It was estimated, however, that he could make as much as $250 million from his share of merchandise sales and other profit incentives, such as bonuses for the number of tickets the Galaxy sold. In an interview in Madrid relayed by satellite to the United States, Beckham said he wanted the chance to help the sport that had given him so much:

> I'm not saying me coming to the States is going to make soccer the biggest sport in America. But if I didn't believe that I could make a difference and take soccer to a different level, then I wouldn't be doing this.[86]

Some sportswriters criticized the huge contract and claimed the Galaxy wanted the thirty-two-year-old Beckham only for his fame, which would boost team profits, and not for his playing ability, which was fading as he grew older. There was

Future Beckham Stars?

When Brooklyn Beckham was born in 1998, gamblers began betting on whether he would ever play professional soccer like his father. Beckham has been happy to teach all three of his sons the game he loves and has said he would not mind those bets coming true:

> I'd love all three of them to become footballers. That would be amazing. But I know how hard it is to get to a high level of playing in football. We are very strict with Brooklyn and we make sure he is polite when he goes to training. I'm biased of course, but I think we have brought him up well and taught him what is important. There are a lot of other distractions out there like computer games but any chance he gets he plays football. Considering he is only seven, he did 17 keepy-uppies [keeping the ball in the air by kicking it] the other day and that's good skill for a boy his age. He loves scoring goals and hitting the ball as hard as he can into the goals. He has got a hell of a strike on him. There's a long, long way for him and the other two to go but all I want is for them to enjoy the game and then after that, we'll see what happens.

Oliver Holt, "Victoria Has Been My Rock," *Daily Mirror* (London), September 18, 2006, p. 4.

some truth to that. In just forty-eight hours after Beckham signed is contract, the Galaxy sold five thousand season tickets, a quarter of its previous year's attendance, and when he joined the team in July, fans in one week purchased more than two hundred thousand replicas of his jersey to make it the world's top selling uniform.

But the Galaxy also wanted Beckham for his soccer skills, which he almost had been unable to showcase in his final

Beckham speaks with his son Brooklyn after a training session.

season with Real Madrid. Fabio Capello, the team's new coach, was so angry that Beckham was leaving that in January he said he would not allow him to play. When the team struggled without Beckham, he began playing him. Capello said that Beckham was key to winning the La Liga championship: "I admit I got that wrong. I think bringing him back was one of the most important influences in the way we have come back and claimed the title."[87]

"The Circus Comes to Town"

After helping Real win the championship, Beckham took a vacation with his family. During that period, coverage about his impending move to Los Angeles saturated the U.S. news media. Alexi Lalas, Galaxy's president, gleefully predicted that when Beckham finally arrived "It's going to be a circus, but it is fun when the circus comes to town."[88] Lalas relished the media coverage because the sport usually received little attention from U.S. newspapers and radio and, television stations.

On July 13, Beckham and his family were introduced to five thousand Galaxy fans in a news conference held outside the team's training facility in Carson, California, a Los Angeles suburb. Not long after Beckham began speaking, he accidentally referred to soccer as football. He immediately apologized, saying, "I've called it football my whole life. Calling it soccer is not a problem for me. Well, at the moment it is because I keep getting it mixed up, but at some point I'll get it after a few weeks."[89] The worshipful crowd laughed off Beckham's language error and accepted his apology.

The "circus" Lalas boasted about included commercials for Adidas that Beckham made with football star Reggie Bush that compared soccer to football. Bush said he knew soccer was a major sport in other countries. "What soccer is to Europe, I think that's what American football is to America,"[90] he said. The media blitz included stories about Victoria, who was still famous as Posh Spice. She even starred on July 16 in *Victoria Beckham: Coming to America*, an NBC television special. She also made headlines in June when she and the other Spice Girls announced they would

Beckham holds up his new jersey during a press conference introducing him to Galaxy fans.

begin performing again. Victoria said she was returning to singing because "I want my kids to see Mommy on the stage doing what I used to do and I want David to see it again."[91] It was the group's first reunion since 2000.

The media did stories about how "Posh and Becks" was one of the world's most famous couples as well as their friendship with actors like Tom Cruise. Also drawing attention was their new $22 million home in Beverly Hills, which was nicknamed "Beckingham Palace West."

To Beckham, however, the only thing that mattered was his effort to raise the status of soccer in the United States. It was something other foreign stars had tried and failed to do in the past.

A Season Shortened by Injury

In the 1970s teams from the North American Soccer League (NASL) signed England's George Best, Germany's Franz Beckenbauer, Holland's Johan Cruyff, and Brazil's Edson Arantes do Nascimento, who is better known as Pele, the greatest soccer player ever. Pele played for the New York Cosmos from 1975 to 1977 and in 1977 he led the team to the Soccer Bowl championship. The league eventually died despite the parade of stars; the MLS, its successor, was founded in 1996.

Like the Galaxy with Beckham, the Cosmos had signed Pele for his ability to attract fans as well as his incredible soccer skills. When Pele was with New York, the league's overall average attendance never hit fifteen thousand even though as many as forty thousand spectators sometimes turned out just to see Pele play. As they had done for Pele three decades earlier, U.S. soccer fans flocked to see Beckham. However, they did not get to watch him play until July 21, when he made his delayed debut before a sold-out crowd of twenty-seven thousand at the Galaxy stadium in Carson during an exhibition game against Chelsea, an English team. Beckham had been unable to compete before then because of his injured left ankle, which had been bothering him since his final weeks with Real.

Beckham made his debut as a Los Angeles Galaxy player on July 21, 2007 during an exhibition game.

The injury sidelined Beckham from MLS games until August 10, when he played thirteen minutes against DC United in Washington, D.C., and he did not score a goal until August 15 in a 2–0 victory at home over United. In New York against the Red Bulls on August 18, Beckham set up two goals in a 5–4 win before 66,237 spectators, most of whom had come only to see him play. The fans cheered and applauded Beckham every time he touched the ball.

As soon as the game was over, Beckham left for England to play for its national team in an August 22 exhibition game against Germany. Germany won 2–1 but Beckham played well for the entire ninety minutes. It was his ninety-seventh game representing England, and Beckham loved it: "When you play for your national team, it means so much."[92] Beckham immediately flew to Los Angeles after the game, and only thirty hours later on Thursday night played ninety minutes again in the Galaxy's 3–0 win over Chivas.

Beckham's international soccer marathon had shown the world that he was still a fine player. However, on August 29 he sprained his right knee in an MLS game against Pachuca. The injury and his still ailing ankle sidelined him from MLS play until October 18, when he got back into action to help the Galaxy tie the New York Red Bulls 1–1. He played in only one more game after that before the Galaxy's season ended on October 21 with a 1–0 loss to Chicago.

Los Angeles, which had such high hopes when Beckham arrived, finished its season with a dismal 9–14–7 record, third worst in the league. Although Beckham was frustrated he had not been able to help his team win more games because of his injuries, he was glad he had been able to get more people interested in soccer:

I never had so many injuries in a short space of time. It's been tough [going from where] I used to play every day in Europe to missing half of the season. . . . We've created the buzz we wanted to around the league. We've had a full house in most of the stadiums we've played in. From that

A David Beckham Interview

Hundreds of newspapers and magazines ran articles about David Beckham when he arrived in the United States in June 2007 to play for the Los Angeles Galaxy. Here are Beckham quotes from one interview:

> I'm not a player like Pele, who would run past five players and score five goals. My qualities [as a player] are the assists and working hard and the free kicks.

> The love of basketball, football, baseball will always be there. But for the biggest sporting nation in the world to not have soccer be big [important] is quite incredible. That's what I want to try and build up.

> It's [Major League Soccer] a lot stronger a league than people who don't know it would think. [In games] I saw talented and hungry players. People will start noticing.

> Each one [tattoo] has a meaning to my career or my life. I don't just go into a shop and pick one out. I have friends who do that, and they're always regretting it 10 years after.

Marco della Cava, "A Taste of Beckham; The Los Angeles Galaxy's New Star Tries to Stay Grounded in Celebrity-Obsessed Tinseltown," *USA Today*, July 23, 2007, p. C3.

part it's been a success, but on my side it's been frustrating because I've not been able to [play much].[93]

Beckham generated a great deal of publicity for soccer and attracted tens of thousands of fans to games. Even though Beckham did not arrive until mid-July, the Galaxy led the league in road attendance with an average 28,035 fans per game and drew a club record 24,252 spectators for each of its fifteen home games. Beckham's star power was also on display in an exhibition game on November 4, 2007, to raise money for victims of California wildfires. Beckham played hard in the contest between Galaxy players and Hollywood United, a team of actors and former soccer stars. "Tonight was a friendly match, but I want to win,"[94] said Beckham. He scored a pair of goals against television actor Anthony LaPaglia in a 12–4 Galaxy victory. The event raised nearly eighty thousand dollars in ticket sales and donations.

The injuries and lack of playing time in his first season in the United States, however, were reminders to the thirty-two-year-old Beckham that his playing career was winding down because of his age. And Beckham had already begun to prepare for the day he would quit playing.

Beckham's Future

Beckham has no interest in coaching the sport professionally but he does want to help youngsters learn the game. In 2005 Beckham opened branches of the David Beckham Academy in London and Los Angeles. Beckham wants his academies to teach boys and girls important life lessons as well as soccer, such as the need to work hard, something his own father taught him. Said Beckham, "It's what kids need to know, and it doesn't just apply to football. It applies to everything."[95]

Many people, however, believe that Beckham wants to be more than a soccer mentor after he retires from playing. When Beckham signed with the Galaxy, some commentators claimed he moved to Los Angeles so he and Victoria could go into movies or television. The predictions started coming true when Victoria signed an agreement in July 2007 to make a guest appearance on *Ugly Betty*, a television show. Beckham himself said when he arrived that playing soccer was the only reason he signed with the Galaxy: "I'm not coming there to be a superstar. I'm coming there to play football."[96] However, in November 2007 it was

Beckham poses with children from the Los Angeles area during a skills demonstration. In 2005, Beckham opened the David Beckham Academy in London and Los Angeles.

reported that he would make a movie with rapper Snoop Dogg, a close friend of his. Snoop claimed in a news story that he and Beckham would produce a film. Said Snoop:

> No one would have thought me and my boy David would have anything in common [but] he has the dollars at his disposal and we're talking about putting our money together to do a movie. It's incredibly exciting.[97]

Making a movie would add to Beckham's fame. But it is his dedication to the game he has loved since he was a child that may one day bring Beckham one of his country's greatest honors—a knighthood. Many people believe Beckham is worthy of this royal designation, which would allow him to be called "Sir David Beckham" and his wife "Lady Victoria," because he has done so much for English soccer. Tony Parsons, an English novelist and newspaper columnist, wrote in June 2007 that Beckham deserves the honor:

> A knighthood for Beckham would be fitting recognition for someone who's been a lionheart for England. In an age when it is fashionable to deride patriotism, Beckham is a proud Englishman [who] would sweat blood for his country. No British sportsman of the past half-century has exerted a more powerful influence on Britain's consciousness.[98]

In fact, there are few athletes of the past half-century who have become more famous and revered globally than David Beckham. All one has to do is listen to his admirers chant "There's only one David Beckham" to realize that.

Notes

Introduction: David Beckham: A Soccer Star and World Celebrity

1. John Carlin, *White Angels: Beckham, Real Madrid and the New Football*. New York: Bloomsbury, 2004, p. 1.
2. Ellen Hale, "The Most Famous Athlete in the World (Except in the USA)," *USA Today*, May 9, 2003, p. A1.
3. Matt Haig, *Brand Royalty: How the World's Top 100 Brands Thrive and Survive*. London: Kogan Page, 2004, p. 153.
4. Quoted in Ken Peters, "Soccer Star Gets L.A. Welcome," *Milwaukee Journal Sentinel*, July 14, 2007, p. B6.
5. Quoted in Hale, "The Most Famous Athlete in the World (except in the USA)," p. A1.

Chapter 1: A Young Boy Dreams of Soccer Stardom

6. Quoted in Grant Wahl, "Big Bend," *Sports Illustrated*, June 23, 2003, p. 60.
7. Ted Beckham, "Becks the Unseen Pictures: I'm So Proud of My David," *Daily Mirror* (London), September 19, 2005, p. 2.
8. Quoted in "David Beckham Interview," *FourFourTwo*, www.fourfourtwo.premiumtv.co.uk/page/BigRead/0,,11442~1015 862,00.html.
9. Quoted in Gabriele Marcotti, "David THE Goliath," *Sports Illustrated for Kids*, March 2005, p. 34.
10. Quoted in Catherine O'Brien, "Ted Beckham Tells Our Interviewer About His Devotion to his Footballing Son and His Acceptance That They Are No Longer so Close," *Times* (London), September 23, 2005, p. 1.
11. David Beckham, *David Beckham's Soccer Skills*. New York: HarperCollins, 2006, p. 22.
12. Ted Beckham, "Becks the Unseen Pictures: I'm So Proud of My David," p. 2.

13. David Beckham with Tom Watt, *Both Feet on the Ground: An Autobiography*. New York: HarperCollins, 2004, p. 7.
14. Quoted in "David Beckham Interview."
15. Beckham with Watt, *Both Feet on the Ground*, p. 14.
16. Beckham, *David Beckham's Soccer Skills*, p. 23.
17. Beckham with Watt, *Both Feet on the Ground*, p. 27.
18. Quoted in *Really Bend it Like Beckham: David Beckham's Soccer Skills*. Burbank, CA: Capital Entertainment Enterprise, , 2005. 2 videodiscs (170 minutes).
19. Beckham with Watt, *Both Feet on the Ground*, p. 28.
20. Beckham, *David Beckham's Soccer Skills*, p. 32.
21. Beckham, "Becks the Unseen Pictures: I'm So Proud of My David," p. 2.
22. Beckham, *David Beckham's Soccer Skills*, p. 18.

Chapter 2: A Teenager Becomes a Professional Player

23. Quoted in *Something About Beckham: A Glimpse Into the Life of Soccer's Most Fascinating Player* (DVD). Los Angeles, CA: Delta Entertainment, 2003. (47 minutes).
24. Beckham, "Becks the Unseen Pictures: I'm So Proud of My David," p. 2.
25. Quoted in *Something About Beckham*.
26. Beckham with Watt, *Both Feet on the Ground*, p. 37.
27. Quoted in Chuck Culpepper, "Beckham: From Working-Class Boy to Man U." *Los Angeles Times*, July 9, 2007, p 12.
28. Beckham with Watt, *Both Feet on the Ground*, p. 38.
29. Quoted in *Something About Beckham*.
30. Quoted in Amy Lawrence, *VII: David Beckham*. London: Weidenfeld & Nicolson, 2006, p. 42.
31. Beckham with Watt, *Both Feet on the Ground*, p. 52.
32. Quoted in Fluto Shinzawa, "Beckham's Galaxy, Soccer Ace's Pitch Has Been Huge Hit." *Boston Globe*, August 10, 2007, p. E1.
33. Quoted in "David Beckham: Rise of a Footballer," British Broadcasting Corporation. www.bbc.co.uk/dna/h2g2/A1138600.

34. Beckham with Watt, *Both Feet on the Ground*, p. 71.
35. Quoted in Lawrence, *VII*, p. 28.
36. Beckham, *David Beckham's Soccer Skills*, p. 84.
37. Quoted in "Beckham's Darkest Hour," uefa.com, July 12, 2002. www.uefa.com/news/magazine/kind=32/newsId=27844,html.
38. Quoted in Ian Thomsen, "Scourge of a Nation," *Sports Illustrated*, September 7, 1998, p. 46.
39. Quoted in John Dillon, "Hate Male—Fears Grow over Beckham Backlash as Hoddle Begs: 'Don't Destroy This Player for Our World Cup Failure,'" *Mirror* (London), July 2, 1998, p. 56.
40. Quoted in Matt Driscoll, "Hate Mob Will Make Becks a Lot More Dangerous," *News of the World* (London), July 26, 1998, p. 78.
41. Beckham, *David Beckham's Soccer Skills*, p. 86.

Chapter 3: Beckham Achieves Worldwide Stardom

42. Quoted in Mark McGuinness, "Becks' Hate Campaign Starts Here," *Mirror* (London), August 10, 1998, p. 40.
43. Quoted in Lawrence, *VII*, p. 29.
44. Quoted in Driscoll, "Hate Mob Will Make Becks a Lot More Dangerous," p. 78.
45. Quoted in Thomas Whitaker, "Sick Fans Will Drive My Son Out Says David Beckham's Dad," *Sun* (London), July 14, 1998, p. 40.
46. Quoted in Lawrence, *VII*, p. 30.
47. Beckham with Watt, *Both Feet on the Ground*, p. 101.
48. Quoted in "Written in the Stars, Victoria and David: Meant to Be," British Broadcasting Corporation. www.news.bbc.co.uk/2/hi/special_report/1999/07/99/the_posh_wedding/382038.stm.
49. Beckham with Watt, *Both Feet on the Ground*, p. 123.
50. Quoted in Thomsen, "Scourge of a Nation," p. 30.
51. Quoted in Driscoll, "Hate Mob Will Make Becks a Lot More Dangerous," p. 78.

52. Beckham with Watt, *Both Feet on the Ground*, pp. 151–52.
53. Quoted in Steve Millar, "We Can Rule for Ten Years; United Stars Pledge to Build on Their Euro Night of Triumph," *Mirror* (London), May 28, 1999, p. 64.
54. Beckham with Watt, *Both Feet on the Ground*, p. 205.
55. Quoted in *Really Bend It Like Beckham: David Beckham's Soccer Skills*.
56. Quoted in Louis Gannon, "Becks to the Future," *Mail on Sunday* (London), February 26, 2006, p. 12.

Chapter 4: Celebrity Royalty: "Posh and Becks"

57. Beckham with Watt, *Both Feet on the Ground*, p. 128.
58. Quoted in Lawrence Donegan, "Woods Places His Sporting Fame Below Brand Beckham," *Guardian* (London), August 8, 2007, p. 34.
59. Spice Girls, *Real Life = Real Spice: The Official Story*. London, England: Azone/VCI, 1997, p. 129.
60. Beckham with Watt, *Both Feet on the Ground*, p. 169.
61. Quoted in "Magazine First for David Beckham," *Daily Mail* (London), April 23, 2002, p. 26.
62. Quoted in "David Beckham Interview."
63. Quoted in Marco della Cava, "A Taste of Beckham; The Los Angeles Galaxy's New Star Tries to Stay Grounded in Celebrity-Obsessed Tinseltown." *USA Today*, July 23, 2007, p. C3.
64. Quoted in Wahl, "Big Bend," p. 64.
65. Quoted in Stephen Moyes and Fiona Cummins, "Exclusive: My David by Ted Beckham," *Daily Mirror* (London), September 20, 2005, p. 12.
66. Quoted in Gannon, "Becks to the Future," p. 12.
67. Quoted in Beth Harris, "Victoria Beckham Downplays Celebrity Status; Former Posh Spice Girl Shields Kids from Media," *Grand Rapids Press* (Michigan), July 11, 2007, p. F10.
68. Quoted in "Beckham: I'll Keep My Family Safe," *Daily Post* (Liverpool), November 4, 2002, p. 2.
69. Quoted in Brian Flynn, "We Live in Terror," *Sun* (London), April 26, 2003, p. 7.

70. Quoted in Marie O'Riordan, "David Beckham—Father, Lover, Icon, Hero," *Marie Claire*, May 2002, p. 62.

71. Quoted in "David Beckham Interview."

72. Quoted in Christian Gysin, "The Day Beckham Turned into Captain Cantankerous," *Daily Mail* (London), May 26, 2004, p. 7.

73. Quoted in Scott Radley, "Becca Loses Cancer Battle; Soccer Superstar Beckham Sends Family His Regrets," *Toronto Star*, January 31, 2007, p. B1.

74. Quoted in Justyn Barnes, "Most Wanted," *Manchester United*, June 2003, p. 40.

Chapter 5: Beckham Stars in Spain and the United States

75. Quoted in "Soccer's Golden Boy," *Evening Mail* (Birmingham, England), May 16, 2000, p. 6.

76. Quoted in Wahl, "Big Bend," p. 60.

77. Quoted in Lawrence, *VII*, p. 38.

78. Quoted in Grahame L. Jones, "He Gives Beckham the Boot," *Los Angeles Times*, February 18, 2003, p. D3.

79. Quoted in Carlin, *White Angels*, p. 40.

80. Quoted in Ben Jackson, "Beckham: 'It Got So Bad I Was Ready to Quit Football,'" *Sun* (London), August 29, 2003, p. 1.

81. Quoted in Carlin, *White Angels*, p. 63.

82. Quoted in Jackson, "Beckham: 'It Got So Bad I Was Ready to Quit Football,'" p. 1.

83. Quoted in Carlin, *White Angels*, p. 90.

84. Quoted in Michelle Kaufman, "Beckham's Popularity Transcends the Game," *Miami Herald*, June 21, 2003, p. 1.

85. Quoted in Paul Logothetis, "Beckham Ends Era on High," *Salt Lake Tribune*, June 18, 2007, p. 1.86. Quoted in Grant Wahl, "Vend It Like Beckham," *Sports Illustrated*, January 22, 2007, p. 16.

87. Quoted in Douglas Robson, "Beckham Bows Out in Spain with Title," *USA Today*, June 18, 2007, p. C3.

88. Quoted in Gary Andrew Poole, "The Beckham Circus Comes to Town," July 8, 2007. www.time.com/time/nation/article/0,8599,1641104,00.html.

89. Quoted in Ken Peters, "Soccer Star Gets L.A. Welcome," *Milwaukee Journal Sentinel*, July 14, 2007, p. B6.

90. Quoted in "One Man's Football Is nother's Futbol," *Greensboro News Record*, July 2, 2007, p. C2.

91. Quoted in Harris, "Victoria Beckham Downplays Celebrity Status; Former Posh Spice Girl Shields Kids from Media," p. F10.

92. Quoted in della Cava, "A Taste of Beckham; The Los Angeles Galaxy's New Star Tries to Stay Grounded in Celebrity-Obsessed Tinseltown," p. C3.

93. Quoted in Beth Harris, "Beckham's Season Ends Prematurely," *Record* (Bergen County, NJ), October 23, 2007, p. S10.

94. Quoted in Billy Witz, "Beckham Not in a Friendly Mood," *Los Angeles Daily News*, November 5, 2007, p. 1.

95. Quoted in Louise Gannon, "Becks to the Future," p. 12.

96. Quoted in "Beckham Is Focused on Soccer, Not Celebrity," *Orlando Sentinel*, January 13, 2007, p. C3.

97. Quoted in Eva Simpson and Caroline Hedley, "Dogg's a Man's Becks Friend!" *Daily Mirror* (London), November 1, 2007, p. 13.

98. Quoted in Kim Murphy, "Sir Becks? Maybe. But Lady Posh? Idea of knighthood for David Beckham makes some Britons uneasy?? a title for his ex-Spice Girl wife, queasy." Los Angeles Times, June 15, 2007, p. A3.

Important Dates

May 2, 1975

David Robert Joseph Beckham is born in Leytonstone, England.

December 1986

Beckham wins the Bobby Charlton Soccer Skills Competition as an eleven-year-old; a Manchester United scout contacts Beckham for the first time.

May 2, 1989

On his fourteenth birthday, Beckham signs schoolboy forms with Manchester United.

July 8, 1991

Beckham, sixteen years old, joins Manchester United as a trainee.

September 23, 1992

Beckham makes his debut for Manchester against Brighton in a 0–0 tie.

January 22, 1993

Beckham, seventeen years old, signs his first professional contract.

December 7, 1994

Beckham scored his first goal for Manchester in a 4–0 win over Galatasaray.

August 17, 1996

Beckham makes a shot from the halfway line, which is 60 yards (55m) from the goal, in a game against Wimbledon. It is nick-named the Wonder Lob and Beckham's fame begins.

September 1, 1996

Beckham plays in a 3–0 win over Moldava in his first game as a member of England's national team.

June 30, 1998

Beckham is given a red card and ejected from the World Cup game against Argentina for kicking Diego Simeone; Beckham is blamed for England's loss in that game.

1999

Beckham leads Manchester United to titles in the Premier League, Football Association Cup, and Champions League.

March 4, 1999

Brooklyn Joseph Beckham is born.

July 4, 1999

Beckham marries Victoria Adams (Posh Spice).

November 15, 2000

Beckham is named captain of England's national team.

September 1, 2002

Romeo James Beckham is born.

July 1, 2003

Beckham signs a four-year contract with Real Madrid.

February 20, 2005

Cruz David Beckham is born.

July 13, 2007

Beckham makes his first public appearance as a member of the Los Angeles Galaxy.

For More Information

Books

David Beckham, *David Beckham: My Side*. London: HarperCollinsWillow, 2002. One of two autobiographies written by Beckham.

Ted Beckham, *David Beckham: My Son*. London: Boxtree, 2005. Beckham's father explains how he helped his son learn to become a great soccer player.

Anna Louise Golden, *The Spice Girls*. New York: Ballantine, 1997. A solid account of how the group got together, with emphasis on the lives of each Spice Girl.

Andrew Morton, *Posh and Becks*. New York: Simon Spotlight Entertainment, 2007. An informative look at one of the world's most famous couples—David and Victoria "Posh Spice" Beckham.

Jill C. Wheeler, *David Beckham*. Edina, MN: ABDO, 2007. A biography of Beckham for the younger reader.

Periodical

Soccer America. A weekly magazine about U.S. and international soccer that has been published since 1970, it is one of the most influential and authoritative periodicals about all levels of the sport from youth to professional soccer. *Soccer America*, 1144 65th Street, Suite F, Oakland, CA 94608. www.socceramerica.com.

Web Sites

Beckham Magazine (www.beckham-magazine.com). An online fan magazine about David Beckham that includes many types of media and information on Beckham.

Beckham Watch (www.beckhamwatch.com). A fan site that includes stories, pictures, videos, news, and other information on David Beckham.

David Beckham (www.davidbeckham.com). David Beckham's official Web site contains news stories, blogs, a biography, photographs, and links to other Internet sites about the soccer star.

David Beckham Academy (www.thedavidbeckhamacademy. com). This Web site has information on Beckham's soccer academies in England and the United States.

Los Angeles Galaxy (http://web.mlsnet.com/t106). The Web site of the major soccer league team Beckham plays for has stories and photos about Beckham as well as links to other information about him.

Soccer America (www.socceramerica.com). The Web site for this weekly magazine about U.S. and international soccer has daily stories about youth, collegiate, and professional soccer as well as links to other news sources about the sport.

About the Author

Michael V. Uschan has written more than 60 books including *Life of an American Soldier in Iraq*, for which he won the 2005 Council for Wisconsin Writers Juvenile Nonfiction Award. It was the second time he won the award. Uschan began his career as a writer and editor with United Press International, a wire service that provided stories to newspapers, radio, and television. Journalism is sometimes called "history in a hurry." Uschan considers writing history books a natural extension of the skills he developed during his many years as a journalist. He and his wife, Barbara, reside in the Milwaukee suburb of Franklin, Wisconsin.